The Art of Talking to Anyone

Other books by Rosalie Maggio

How to Say It
How to Say It Style Guide
The New Beacon Book of Quotations by Women
Talking About People
Marie Marvingt: Femme d'un Siècle
The Music Box Christmas
How They Said It
Great Letters for Every Occasion
Money Talks
An Impulse to Soar
Quotations on Love
Quotations for the Soul
Quotations on Education
Quotations From Women on Life
The Dictionary of Bias-Free Language
The Nonsexist Word Finder
The Travels of Soc

The Art of Talking to Anyone

Essential People Skills for Success in Any Situation

Rosalie Maggio

McGraw-Hill

New York   Chicago   San Francisco   Lisbon   London
Madrid   Mexico City   Milan   New Delhi
San Juan   Seoul   Singapore
Sydney   Toronto

The **McGraw·Hill** Companies

Copyright © 2005 by Rosalie Maggio. All rights reserved. Printed in the United States of America. Except as permitted under the United States Copyright Act of 1976, no part of this publication may be reproduced or distributed in any form or by any means, or stored in a data base or retrieval system, without the prior written permission of the publisher.

18 19 20   QFR/QFR   1 5 4 3

ISBN 978-0-07-145229-8
MHID 0-07-145229-X

This publication is designed to provide accurate and authoritative information in regard to the subject matter covered. It is sold with the understanding that neither the author nor the publisher is engaged in rendering legal, accounting, or other professional service. If legal advice or other expert assistance is required, the services of a competent professional person should be sought.

—*From a Declaration of Principles jointly adopted by Committee of the American Bar Association and a Committee of Publishers.*

McGraw-Hill books are available at special quantity discounts to use as premiums and sales promotions, or for use in corporate training programs. For more information, please write to the Director of Special Sales, McGraw-Hill Professional, Two Penn Plaza, New York, NY 10121-2298. Or contact your local bookstore.

Library of Congress Cataloging-in-Publication Data

Maggio, Rosalie.
The art of talking to anyone : essential people skills for success in any situation / Rosalie Maggio.
    p.   cm.
Includes index.
ISBN 0-07-145229-X (alk. paper)
1. Interpersonal communication.   I. Title.
HM1166.M34   2005
646.7'6—dc22

2005000247

To DAVID
Liz, Katie, Matt, Nora

Contents

Introduction   ix

Part One: The Basics   1

Chapter 1: How to Succeed in Any Conversation: From Start to Finish   3

Chapter 2: How to Be Universally Liked   23

Chapter 3: How to Listen Successfully   31

Chapter 4: How to Keep a Conversation Going—or Stop One   37

Chapter 5: How to Ask and Answer Questions   45

Chapter 6: How and When to Tell Jokes   55

Chapter 7: How to Deal With Conversational Predicaments   61

Chapter 8: How to Be an Unpopular Conversationalist   75

Part Two: The Specifics   97

Chapter 9: Talking With Anyone in the Workplace   99

Chapter 10: Talking With Anyone at Meetings and Conferences   115

Chapter 11: Talking With Anyone at Business-Social Events   129

Chapter 12: Talking With Anyone at Social Events   139

Chapter 13: Talking With Anyone in Public Places   155

Chapter 14: Talking With Anyone on the Telephone   165

Chapter 15: Talking With Anyone in Times of Trouble   179

Chapter 16: Talking With Family and Friends   191

Chapter 17: Talking With Romance in Mind   203

Index   217

Introduction

> *There is no reason why any one of us cannot become a good conversationalist. ... It is universal and it is one of the most decisive factors in our success or failure.*
>
> —Lillian Eichler

If you have picked up this book, you most likely believe that being able to converse fluently and appropriately is a key factor in your workplace success and your personal happiness. You don't need to be convinced of its importance. *The Art of Talking to Anyone* rests on this shared understanding and offers you not the *why* of conversation, but the *how*.

The assumption here is that you can already converse—you've been doing it most of your life—and that you are a much better conversationalist than you realize. But you are, if not a perfectionist, at least a striver, and you want to be better.

The Art of Talking to Anyone will prime your pump, jump-start your battery, provide the inspiration you need to attain absolute confidence in your ability to say the right thing to anyone, anytime, anywhere.

Part One is your toolbox. Guidelines and strategies provide you with everything you need to become a more successful conversationalist: What is a good question? When should you not tell a joke? How do you get away from a nonstop talker? What verbal tics might you unknowingly have? How do you respond to a rude question? How, exactly, do you introduce two people to each other?

Part Two offers practical help making conversation in nine areas of your life. Each chapter includes suggestions on what to say, what not to say, what to do in special circumstances, and how you might handle various situations. The section "If They Say... You Say..." illustrates the back-and-forth nature of talking with others.

No one says being a well-liked and charming conversationalist is easy. More than a hundred years ago, Gamaliel Bradford confessed, "Somehow I find talk very unsatisfactory. I never say the things I meant to say and am overwhelmed afterwards with the things I should have said and could not." Sound familiar?

Someone once asked a friend, "How did you get to be really good at making conversation?" The friend replied, "By experience." "Oh?" asked the other. "And how did you get your experience?" The friend said dryly, "From being really bad at making conversation."

The Art of Talking to Anyone will save you from having to make bad conversation on your way to becoming a self-assured, sought-after, successful conversationalist.

The Art of Talking to Anyone

Part One

The Basics

CHAPTER 1

How to Succeed in Any Conversation: From Start to Finish

> *Good manners—the longer I live the more convinced I am of it—are a priceless insurance against failure and loneliness. And anyone can have them.*
>
> —ELSA MAXWELL

Before Talking With Anyone

The art of conversing with anyone begins long before you arrive at wherever you hope to speak charmingly and intelligently. This chapter tells you what you need to know for every step of a conversation, from introductions to body language to ending the conversation gracefully.

Convince Yourself You Want to Go

The first step is to choose to be there. If it's the workplace, you are allowed to feel ambiguous about your decision some mornings, but to make a good impression—at work, at a meeting, at a party, or at any kind of gathering—go with a positive attitude.

If you hate being someplace, you can imagine that your conversation will not be scintillating. So either take your happy face with you or stay home. If you are attending something unwillingly because of

> *Positive people can take on the world.*
>
> —RICK PITINO

work or family obligations, remember that a good attitude and a bad attitude are simply different ways of looking at the same situation. Your choice.

Have Something to Say

Don't leave home without it: something to say. Chances are you read a daily newspaper, perhaps a weekly newsmagazine, and, if you belong to that particular 53% of the U.S. population, a book now and then. Collect fodder for conversation from the radio, friends, sermons, lectures, public television, eavesdropping on the subway, or waiting in line at the grocery store. Keeping up with current events and popular culture ensures you'll never be caught short in the conversation sweepstakes.

You won't, of course, baldly drop whatever you know into the conversation. When you feel the need to break a silence, start with a question: "Did you see the article in this morning's paper about...?" "Has anyone read Stephen King's latest?" If there is no interest in your gambit, try something else or hope another person in the group has been doing their homework.

You might keep a list of conversation topics—activities that interest you, questions, ideas—and review them before leaving for a social or business event. You might not need them, but you'll feel better knowing you can hold your own if you have to.

If you can, find out a little about those who will be attending the event. That information plus three or four conversational tidbits should see you through almost any situation. But don't even think about rehearsing possible "conversations." The irregular nature of most conversations makes them unpredictable, and you'll look stilted besides.

Take Your Best Self With You

The single most important element in being the kind of person everyone wants to talk with is...confidence. You want to walk into a room, comfortable in the knowledge that you are happy to be there, that you're looking forward to meeting some interesting people, and that you can handle whatever conversational challenges come your way.

Expect to be liked and accepted. Take for granted that people will be happy to see you. And what's not to like? You were invited, you're part of this group, you're a good person.

The three principles behind looking, acting, and being confident are:

1. People will take you at your own evaluation. Your attitudes about yourself bounce back to you from other people. If you think you

> *People, in forming their opinions of others, are usually lazy enough to go by whatever is most obvious or whatever chance remark they happen to hear. So the best policy is to dictate to others the opinion you want them to have of you.*
> —Judith Martin

have no social skills, other people will eventually come to agree with you. If you think you have nothing to say, you certainly will have nothing to say, and people will start seeing you as someone who has nothing to say. If you think you are a nobody, you are practically asking people to treat you that way. On the other hand, if you think of yourself as a kind, intelligent, charming person, that's the way you'll be perceived.

2. People will catch and mirror your emotional states. If you are enthusiastic, they will be too; if you are bored, they will also be bored.

3. People tend to behave the way you think they will behave. If you think people are cold and snooty, they will probably end up acting that way to you. If you think they look down on you, ultimately they probably will. But if you think people are interesting, warm, and funny, they will not make a liar of you. If you expect people to accept you, they will.

People will know if your attitude is defensive and insecure, or if it is relaxed and open. They might not think it through, but at some level, whatever you think, feel, and project will be picked up by others and returned to you.

Because the aim of small talk is to make people comfortable and to put them at their ease, a self-conscious, tense, nervous conversationalist is going to be socially inadequate.

> *All power is based on perception. If you think you've got it, then you've got it. If you think you don't have it, even if you have it, then you don't have it.*
> —Herb Cohen

You have doubts. By some magic, you are expected to go from a social shipwreck to a conversational Queen Mary?

The magic is to "act as if." Act as if you are brave and confident. Act as if others are happy to see you. You've got to believe—or at least act as though you believe—that the other person is going to enjoy spending a few minutes with you.

It might feel artificial at first, but the more you "act as if," the more the new behaviors will begin to feel comfortable. Keep reminding yourself that the vast majority of any group is kind, well mannered, and willing to give anyone a chance. Even a second chance.

Feel free to be thinking, "Help! I'm a fish out of water! I'm going to die. I don't know what to say! I'm boring! Nobody is interested in me! I'm going to spill something! They're going to discover I'm a fraud!" Think anything you like—but stand up straight, smile, shake hands, and calmly and charmingly say, "It's a pleasure to meet you."

Remember this: You are not everyone's cup of tea. It's simply not possible that every individual at a gathering will want to marry you, be your best friend, or share an office with you. What would you do with that many people in your life anyway? So most people you speak with will provide low-key, pleasant conversation, but you don't need to be a "hit" with everyone. You do not need to be perfect. The desire for perfection, for doing things absolutely "right," has been the downfall of many a good conversationalist. Relax. In the end, this or that small conversation doesn't matter in the large scheme of things.

> *Nothing is more essential to success in any area of your life than the ability to communicate well.*
> —PAUL W. SWETS

You'll be more popular, and thus probably happier, if you concentrate on making the other person feel good. You can't make anyone like you, but it's in your power to show liking for others.

Check Out Your Body Language

From the moment you walk in the door, your body is busy telling people all about you.

What would you think about someone who rushed into a gathering, looking harried and slightly sweaty? Or someone who slouched in furtively, hoping not to be noticed? Or someone who had "apologetic" written all over them, from hunched shoulders to puppy-dog eyes? You probably wouldn't be anxious to talk with that person. Think about the image you want to project. Shouldn't it be one of confidence?

Posture   With any luck, you already have good posture. It's distracting to be trying to converse with people while simultaneously hissing to yourself, "Stand up straight!" "Shoulders back!" "Stomach in!" If your posture needs work, work on it before and after, not during, events that call for conversation. Self-consciousness will prevent you from being the interesting person you can be.

> *Movement never lies.*
> —MARTHA GRAHAM

The person who stands tall—but not stiffly—and moves in a calm, purposeful way automatically commands respect. From the moment you enter a room with dignity and easy confidence, you tell people you are someone who matters—to yourself and to them.

Good posture includes the way you hold your head. Study the way people in your life carry their heads and see what you think of the differences.

In general, keep your head level (the metaphor "level head" did not spring from nowhere). A level head indicates an assured, candid, capable nature. It might also give your voice fuller tones and make you seem to be looking people straight in the eye.

A bowed head, eyes studying the floor, makes you look unsure, vulnerable, passive, and possibly even guilty of something.

Tilting your head to one side or the other (most people tilt to the right), may show curiosity and interest. But it may also indicate unease, helplessness, dependence, or bewilderment.

Fidgeting and Gestures

Some body language is difficult to control:

- Blushing
- Contraction of facial muscles
- Involuntary grimaces
- Rapid blinking

Working on your self-confidence and your comfort level is the only cure for these types of reflexes. They will disappear when you begin to see yourself as an able and resourceful conversationalist.

Other body language can be controlled with practice:

- Adjusting your eyeglasses
- Clearing your throat constantly
- Crossing your arms tightly over your chest
- Fiddling with a pen, purse, or other object

- Fidgeting
- Fingering rings or jewelry
- Folding and unfolding your arms
- Giggling
- Glancing continually at your watch
- Hitching up your belt
- Laughing nervously or too loudly
- Looking around the room
- Making distracting gestures
- Picking lint from your clothes
- Playing with your tie
- Pocketing your hands
- Pushing back, flipping, smoothing, or fluffing your hair
- Rocking on your feet, side-to-side, or forwards and backwards
- Scratching your head or chin
- Slouching or leaning
- Smoothing your clothing
- Tucking in bra or slip straps
- Tugging at shirt cuffs
- Twisting a mustache

> *I never look at my watch if I'm talking with someone. I think that's such an insulting gesture! It suggests you're trying to gauge whether you think what they're saying is worth your time.*
> —FRANCES HESSELBEIN

The first step is to be aware of what you're doing; most of these behaviors belong to people who have no idea they're fidgeting. Repetitive and pointless gestures spring from nervousness and insecurity. Once you begin gaining confidence in your skills and popularity as a conversationalist, it will be fairly easy to weed them out.

An unnerving trait in a conversational partner is distractibility. Don't let your attention wander from the other person to the loudly dressed individual across the room or the inexplicable choice of art on the walls or the entrance of newcomers or the conversation going on next to you. Ignore everything but the people with whom you're conversing.

Other body language to be avoided includes:

- ▶ Shaking, waving from side to side, or pointing your forefinger at another person (this is an incredibly aggressive and unwelcome gesture—there are other ways to punctuate your remarks).
- ▶ Standing too closely to someone. The preference for personal space varies, but it is important to some people. The best way to handle this is to keep your distance; let the other person move toward you. This is psychologically a good strategy, both in showing respect to the other person and in the other person demonstrating their "attraction" to you by moving closer.

In moderation, gestures are appreciated as long as they are not always the same gesture. After checking the list above for the fidgeting kinds of gestures, use any others that feel natural to you.

If you travel to other countries, familiarize yourself with the social and business customs there. For example, in the United States the "okay" sign (the O with forefinger and thumb) means money in Japan, and in Italy and Latin America can be insulting. Patting a child on the head is considered a benign, even charming gesture in many countries; in Islamic countries it must be strictly avoided because the head is the holiest part of the body and not to be touched. A number of books, including several good series, detail cultural issues for visitors to other countries.

> *"Be yourself" is good advice, unless you notice that people are always excusing themselves and moving away from you. In that case, try being someone else!*
> —SUSAN ROANE

Smile! All that said, you might be wondering what physical movements are left to you. The best ones are a good smile and an occasional, meaningful nod. Senseless and too-frequent nodding is the opposite of the infrequent, thoughtful nod, which tells people you are involved in what they're saying.

But the smile—oh, the smile will work miracles. It is the most important body language of all, signaling that you are affable, comfortable in your skin, and receptive to whoever the other person might be. The tendency of the human being is to reflect the

> *Top people smile more frequently than people on any other rung of the career ladder—and not just because they make more money.*
> —D.A. BENTON

emotion the other person displays. If you smile, chances are very good the other person will smile back.

In some people, the smile is almost an involuntary tic. They smile regardless of the content of what they're saying. However, if this is you, before you start trying to fix it, remember that there are lots worse things we can see on people's faces than a smile.

There must be some smiles that are not desirable—the insincere smile, the strained smile—but anyone trying to smile for whatever reason should be given a chance to come up with a real smile. Any smile is probably a good smile.

Introductions

Although there are rules for introducing one person to another, don't worry if they suddenly fly out of your head. Instead of being seized with horror and trying to remember what you "ought" to do, simply trust yourself, treat both people with liking and respect, and figure out a way for each of them to know the other's name. It isn't much more complicated than that.

- ▶ To introduce two people: (1) give their full names and (2) add an impersonal identifying tag such as:

 "A dear friend of mine"

 "My business partner"

 "My neighbor in the next condo"

 "My niece Susan"

 "The new architect with our company"

By adding a tagline, you give the two people a place to begin a conversation ("How long have you lived in this building?" "Do you live in town, or are you visiting?"). Do not attach embarrassing or excessive tags ("I used to change his diapers when he was little"; "She's the best pumpkin-pie maker in the country today"). If you know that the two people have something in common (they both recently traveled to Peru; they both collect paperweights; they both know your brother), mention it.

- ▶ The part of introductions that generally is a challenge is deciding (quickly) who gets introduced to whom. The formula is:

 "Mother, I'd like you to meet Little Jack Horner."

 "Jack, this is my mother, Ima Goose."

Although we think we're an egalitarian society, one person is usually ranked a little more highly than the other. That person gets to find out first who the other person is. The higher-ranked person is on the left:

senior executive	junior executive
older neighbor	younger neighbor
clergy	nonclergy
professor	student
adult	child
manager	employee
longtime friend	someone you met last week

For the first person, use the name you are accustomed to using. If you introduce your boss to someone, depending on your place in the organization, you might say, "Ms. George, I'd like you to meet my wife, June Olson." Each introduction is a little different from every other one. However, the samples below demonstrate in a general way how effective introductions work:

> *Courtesy is the bedrock of social interchange.*
> —JOAN M. DRURY

"Anna, do you know Bob Lorimer? Ah, good, then I get to introduce you. Bob is a translator with Pelham Oil. Bob, this is Anna Pierson, also a translator, but with Guest & Company."

"Dad, I'd like you to meet a friend of mine, Joni Kessell. Joni, this is my father, Arnold Dombey. Yes, the geology professor himself! Dad, Joni is majoring in geology and she's always wanted to meet you."

"Eden, you've heard me talk about Farley Novak. Farley, this is my good friend and colleague Eden Murchison. I believe you both went to Yale, but at different times."

"I normally hesitate to introduce two of my friends to each other because too often it doesn't seem to work out, but I think this is a special case. Chris, I'd like you to meet Dana Casserly. Dana, this is Chris Deadham, and the reason I thought you'd enjoy meeting is that you are the only two people I know who both speak Farsi!"

"Irene, have you met Frank Cooper? He's my assistant, without whom I couldn't exist. Frank, this is Irene Maundrell, our Manhattan Regional Director."

"Maria, I'd like to introduce you to Ethel Ormiston, who is our very favorite realtor. Ethel, this is Maria Gauss. She and her husband Eugene are going to put their home on the market soon."

"Millicent, this is Hannah Vorbrüggen, an exchange student from Germany. Hannah, I'd like you to meet my sister-in-law, Millicent Cassine. Their children are taking German and Millicent was wondering if you'd have any spare time for tutoring."

"Someone just told me you're making a documentary on Deaf culture and, as someone who has been wishing for just such a documentary, I'd like to introduce myself. My name is David Herries."

- ▶ Although you can just begin speaking with someone without actually introducing yourselves to each other, it's probably not a good idea. By the time you're well into a warm, friendly conversation it's awkward to have to say, "Um, what was your name?"

- ▶ After being introduced, use the other person's title ("Dr. Schneider") or honorific plus last name ("Ms. Arnault") until they suggest you call them by their first name, especially if they are professors, doctors, bosses, or older individuals. Do not use nicknames if the person doesn't use it; Charles is not Chuck and Elizabeth is not Lizzie unless you're so informed. Be careful, too, to use people's names in parallel fashion. It's very telling if you're newly introduced and you address one of your new acquaintances by their first name and the other by their title.

- ▶ In a pinch, you can get people to introduce themselves to each other. Indicate the one you know, even if only by first name, and say, "This is Gene." The other person will reflexively give their name, and Gene will generally supply a last name to round things out. This is not a particularly suave move, but 'twill serve sometimes.

- ▶ Immediately after being introduced, jot the other person's name in your mental Rolodex. Try to associate the name and face in some way, or use the person's name several times during the conversation until you think you've got it. Some people collect business cards; at home they jot notes on the cards so that they can recall the person later.

  Unfortunately, many people run into someone an hour or two later at the same conference or party and, oops! The name is completely gone. See Chapter 7 for some ideas if you forget a name.

- ▶ If you're sitting when someone approaches you with another person in tow, stand up for the introduction that's coming; both women and men do this.

- Note that when used for introductions, the question "How do you do?" is not actually a question. It is a ritual greeting, to which the response (sometimes delivered simultaneously) is "How do you do?" In a variant of this, sometimes you'll see one person saying, "How are you?" The other person responds, "Very well, thank you. And you?" Again, it is simply a formula to ease you through the introduction.
- The biggest no-no in introductions is to approach someone and say, "Do you remember me?"
- When seeing someone you've met before but know only superficially, extend your hand and remind them of your name: "Hello, Ken. Mario DiNardo. Nice to see you again." This allows the other person to say graciously if perhaps not truthfully, "Mario! I know who you are!" It is charming for you to assume that you aren't so famous that everyone knows who you are.

> *Why is it that the person who needs no introduction usually gets the longest one?*
> —MARCELENE COX

- If the other person doesn't offer a name, you can always introduce yourself:

    "Hello, I'm Francine Beauchamp. I'm in accounting on the third floor."

    "Hello, I'm Roland Bemrick, an old classmate of our host."

    "Hello, I'm Sheila Tory and this is my first meeting. Have you been a member very long?"

    "May I introduce myself? I'm Janet Ahlin and I've just moved in down the street. I believe you live in the neighborhood too."

Shaking Hands

Few people need lessons in how to shake hands, but in order for you to feel absolutely confident about this preconversational gesture, here are the guidelines:

- Approach the other person with hand already extended.
- Look them in the eye, and smile slightly. Try to make your look say, "Ah, you are an interesting looking person!"
- Grasp hands, palm to palm, firmly but not tightly. Remember that otherwise healthy-looking individuals might have painful arthritis in

their hands; others might be wearing rings that a too-vigorous handshake will drive into their skin. Try to match the grip of the other person. They will, in turn, be trying to match theirs to yours. In some mysterious way you will usually arrive at a handshake satisfactory to all.

- In some countries, a handshake is a brisk up and down, a one-two maneuver. In other countries, one person's left hand is placed atop the two clasped hands to convey additional warmth. In the United States, people sometimes continue shaking hands for several seconds. In the case of a person one has long wanted to know, the handshake is prolonged, and the use of the other hand is brought into play. The most general advice would be to adapt yourself to the other person's manner unless you have strong feelings of your own about making the handshake a special one.

- While you are shaking hands, you will be looking at the other person's eyes and saying your introductory line (for example, "I'm delighted to meet you at last").

- In most areas of the United States, women and men approach handshakes in exactly the same manner. In some places, women extend their hands first so that the other person knows a handshake is welcome (this might be a remnant of the days in which women were not on an equal social footing with men).

Basic Conversational Principles

You have probably come up with some good conversational principles yourself, even though you might never have spelled them out. Whatever works, works. However, if you're looking to fine-tune your skills, see if anything below resonates with you.

- The goal of the first few minutes of any conversation with someone you don't know is threefold: (1) to find out a few things about the other person, (2) to tell a few things about yourself, (3) to find some common ground between you. Even in a big city, if you talk with anyone for five minutes, you will find several items in common. As Judith Martin ("Miss Manners") puts it, you must forage "for a topic of mutual interest. This is done by putting forth a collection of bland observations until one of them is seized upon and developed."

- The key to a good conversation is a certain back-and-forthing. Englishman Raymond Mortimer once said that in the United States, conversation "is not tennis, in which you return the other fellow's service, but golf, in which you go on hitting your own ball."

Nothing will be more helpful to you in becoming an outstanding conversationalist than this metaphor of a tennis game. Keeping the ball in the air is an art, and the point of most conversations.

> *Conversation is a turn-taking game. You talk, then I talk, then you talk again. One person starts talking when another is finished.*
> —DEBORAH TANNEN

- Vary your contributions to the conversation by alternating among (1) making statements, (2) asking questions, (3) offering a piece of information about yourself, and (4) asking something (not too personal) about the other person. Then start all over again. An agreeable balance among these four elements will produce the best kind of conversation.

- To get started, you might ask the other person about their work or interests or, better yet, volunteer a little of that information about yourself. Keep the tone and the content of the conversation light until you find a topic you are both interested in and want to explore at some depth. Conversational gold is found when you mine a topic you are both passionate about.

- Use the word "you" much more often than you use the word "I." That's not to say that you shouldn't use "I" at all. In the give-and-take of conversation, you need to counter information offered by the other person with some information about yourself. If you are discussing a topic, tell how it relates to you or why you're interested in it. This adds layers to the conversation. But when "I" outweighs "you" in your conversation, you will notice a waning enthusiasm in the other person.

> *I am a firm believer in letting guests start off on commonplaces till they have shaken down and got the temperature of the room. Even the weather, or the climate, is an unfailingly good topic.*
> —ALFRED NORTH WHITEHEAD

- In a group, stimulate conversation as much as you can. Bring in the quiet ones, pass the baton to someone who hasn't spoken, try to discover an interest common to all of you.

- Be interested and friendly, cheerful and good-humored, courteous and flexible, respectful and open-minded. Yes, that's a tall order, but if you go into a conversation expecting good things from it, you'll be all that and more.

▶ Look from person to person and keep a pleasant expression on your face, if your face will do that for you. If you are downhearted or discouraged, unhappy or uncomfortable, try to box the feelings up for later examination. Not only will you be badly out of place in a general conversation, but it really won't do you any good. And the next time people see you, they might feel like hunting up the nearest restroom.

▶ Use the words "we," "our," "ourselves," and "us" to establish a sort of kinship, a sense of being in the same boat.

▶ If you are shy or self-conscious, the best cure is to approach anyone standing alone or someone who has been looking as though they'd like to talk with you but are too reserved to do so. Larry King points out, "The person you're talking to is probably just as shy as you are. Most of us are." At any gathering there is likely to be a handful of guests as ill at ease as you are. Find them. Try not to spend long periods of time with one person, however, even if it is more comfortable for you. Social and business gatherings are not designed for two people to hole up in a corner and ignore everyone else. Mingling is expected of everyone.

▶ Avoid talking while you are eating or drinking. Unless you are very, very hungry or thirsty, or unless you are an old hand at these things, you might want to stay with Perrier and lime (not a problem if you spill it).

▶ Don't worry about showing ignorance of a topic or saying "I don't know," "No, I'm not familiar with that," or "I've never heard of such a thing." Will Rogers pointed out that everyone is ignorant, just on different subjects. You undoubtedly know things the other person doesn't. But a conversation isn't a competition. You're not on *Jeopardy*. You will be liked for saying straight out that you don't know, and then asking the other person to tell you about it.

▶ A good conversationalist uses details, precise descriptions, colorful nouns. The writer Joan Aiken tells about her daughter reading a story in which the main character said, "We went into the chateau and were served with wine and little cakes." Her daughter flung down the magazine, exclaiming, "What's the use of that, if she doesn't tell you what *sort* of little cakes?" Try to always tell what sort of little cakes.

▶ Unless you are in a business discussion, avoid jargon, multisyllabic words, and slang.

▶ Try to establish a feeling that you're on the same wavelength. We tend to feel warm toward people who agree with us. You needn't betray your own principles, but if you fish cleverly enough, you'll pull up something you both find edible.

When appropriate, sprinkle your conversation with brief expressions of kinship: "I'm like that too"; "I've always thought that"; "I agree completely"; "I'm crazy about mine"; "I share your enthusiasm"; "That's exactly what I think." Remember that saying "I'm just like you!" is far more flattering than saying "You're just like me!"

Be careful about seizing on the common bond to wrest the conversation from the other person. Wait to tell about your adventure at Yosemite until they're finished talking about theirs. (See the "Me Too" problem in Chapter 8.)

> *Good manners is the art of making those people easy with whom we converse. Whoever makes the fewest persons uneasy, is the best bred in the company.*
> —JONATHAN SWIFT

▶ You might even attempt to match your rhythm of speaking and the volume of your voice to the other person's. This makes them feel even more that you are in tune with them. It's not a case of being a phony, speaking in a way that isn't natural to you. If you were driving a car with a friend who wanted to watch the scenery, you'd slow down. If the other person was late for an appointment, you'd drive faster; in other words, you'd accommodate them. Do the same for a conversational partner.

▶ There's a reason it's called small talk. With people you don't know well, you want to skate on the surface of the ice—no fair awling holes to get into the deep, cold waters of philosophy, theology, the role of love in fourteenth-century Spain, or how deconstructionists have affected our universities. Unless. Unless someone else starts it, and everyone in your small group wants to discuss it. In that case, you'll have fun. Don't feel you have to contribute something astonishing and unique and outrageous to the conversation. Or even something literary or intellectual or clever. Everyday topics are always acceptable. The key is to be sure everyone is included, and that all are interested.

> *Never try to say something remarkable. It is sure to be wrong.*
> —MARK RUTHERFORD

Eye Contact

If you've ever spoken with someone unable to make eye contact, you remember how disconcerting it is. You are tempted to bend over and float into the range of their vision. If you are uncomfortable making eye contact, practice with family and friends until you are able to maintain eye contact at least half the time when conversing with others. It is an important business and social skill. People who can't meet our eyes suggest nefarious doings, character weaknesses, and perhaps mysterious private activities.

> *His eyes...not only undressed you unblinkingly, but shaved your head, called your parents, and refused to refinance your house.*
>
> —CARRIE FISHER

The best eye contact is direct but not unrelenting. From time to time, look away—or at least over the person's shoulder—so that you don't appear to be memorizing their face. Unrelieved eye contact makes people uncomfortable. It also helps to look at the other person's whole face instead of at just their eyes.

In close-up film scenes, you might notice that a lover looks first at one eye and then at the other eye of the beloved; this makes it more interesting viewing for us, but in real life this is a useful device because it makes you look especially responsive to the other person.

Touching

Some people highly recommend touching those you're conversing with. One expert recommends it so highly that she says, "If you simply cannot bring yourself to touch, at least make an extra effort to convey the message a touch would through your facial expression, tone of voice, and words. But doing this exclusively is gutless."

That's one person's opinion. The recommendation here, however, is that, except for handshakes, you refrain from touching people who are business or social acquaintances. The logic is that you are far more likely to err by touching someone who doesn't welcome it (and uninvited touching feels very aggressive to many people, both women and men) than you are to err by being warm and friendly but limiting yourself to shaking hands.

A person is unlikely to leave you complaining to a friend, "She didn't hug me! What's the matter with her?" However, the person whose space was invaded by an unsought-for touch might well feel ruffled and displeased.

The president of a company says, "When I meet new people, I'll grab their hand, shake it, and give a bear hug by putting my other arm around their shoulder. Their reaction may be catatonic. They may try to take two steps backward. Or they may simply relax and enjoy it. But they don't forget it."

You might make your own decision about how effective touching and bear hugs are, but the discreet, unassailable position is to save your hugs for friends and family.

Mingling

One of the tacit rules about conversing in a business or social gathering is that you move from person to person or from small group to small group so that, in theory at least, you spend a little time with everyone.

For a one-on-one conversation, arrange a coffee or lunch meeting with that person for another time; don't single out one of a number of people for an in-depth chat.

Most people are familiar with the commandment to mingle, so they will be as willing to let you move on as you are to let them.

When you encounter someone who has cornered you and is impervious to a hint, you can free yourself by backing away, while using one of the good-bye lines in the section below.

After Talking With Someone

Bringing a conversation to a close is a paltry thing compared to getting one off the ground. Still, there are conventions to be observed. One does not simply notice the time, grab one's overcoat, and bolt.

Ending a Conversation

Most conversations find their graceful, convenient, and natural end when those involved realize it's time to change partners.

In the event that you are trapped by someone lacking this sensitivity, you need to extricate yourself. Signaling wildly to friends to come to your rescue is unacceptable. Rolling your eyes or being otherwise rude to the long-winded one is not a good idea either. This person was invited and is obviously of interest to your host or to your company, so you don't want to be offensive.

> *You have delighted us long enough.*
> —JANE AUSTEN

What to do? A preventive measure is to always fill your glass only one-quarter full so that you have the excuse of going for a refill.

You can also interrupt yourself, instead of interrupting the other person:

"Our new product line was just taking off when—Omigosh, I should have been somewhere else ten minutes ago. Sorry!"

Or, try a phrase like one of these:

"Before I forget, I need to ask Sonia a question. Will you excuse me?"
"Before we quit here, let me introduce you to a friend of mine."
"By the way, do you know where the restroom is?"
"Can you tell me what time it is? Oh no! Say, excuse me, but I've got to make a call."
"Did you tell Gerry about your project? I think she'd be interested."
"Emma [getting the attention of a passerby], have you met Stuart?"
"Excuse me, I need something to drink. I think I'm coming down with a cold."
"Give my best to your family, will you?"
"Good luck with the project. I'll be watching for news of it."
"How about getting something from the buffet?"
"I'd like you to meet Suresh. Let's go say hello to him."
"I don't want to monopolize you, so I'll let you go meet a few other people."
"I have a question for Pamela about her speech. Do you want to come with me?"
"I haven't even said hello to our hosts yet—will you excuse me?"
"I hope we can do business together at some point. Here's my card."
"I'll call you Monday with that address. Until then, I hope you enjoy the rest of the conference."
"I'll see you at next week's meeting then."
"I'm sorry, but I just remembered something."
"I'm sorry, but I need to take some medication now."
"I'm supposed to take a turn welcoming people at the door, so if you'll excuse me..."
"I'm trying to catch Dr. Sarspen before she leaves—will you excuse me?"

"I need to have a word with someone from my department, and it looks as though he's leaving."

"I see Dylan Chastain. May I introduce you to him?"

"I see some new faces, and I think I'll go meet them. Do you want to come with me?"

"I shouldn't keep you. I know there are other people who want to talk with you."

"I suppose we'd better go mingle."

"I think I'm getting the signal from Jim that it's time to leave."

"It's been a pleasure talking with you [and backing away]."

"It's been great talking with you. Maybe I'll see you later."

"I've been monopolizing you. I'm sure you want to talk with other people here."

"I've enjoyed chatting with you. Maybe our paths will cross again sometime."

"I've enjoyed meeting you and I'll call if I find out anything more about the trade show."

"I want to ask the speaker a question. Would you like to come with me?"

"I want to say a few words to someone who's new to the department."

"I was hoping to meet a few potential clients this afternoon. I should probably get started."

[Shaking hands] "It's been wonderful meeting you!"

"The buffet looks extraordinary. Shall we go see what's over there?"

"The stuffed mushrooms were fabulous. I'm going to get seconds."

"This has been great, but we probably shouldn't neglect everyone else."

"While I'm thinking of it, I should make a phone call."

"Will you excuse me for a minute? I need to check on something."

"Will you excuse me? I'm going to find a restroom."

"Would you excuse me? I just spotted someone I haven't seen in twenty years."

Saying Good-Bye

Shakespeare said it first: "Stand not upon the manner of your going, but go at once."

In small or intimate groups, you will want to say good-bye to each person individually. In larger social or business gatherings, this is neither practical nor desirable. You might, however, write a brief note of thanks in the days following.

Take leave of your hosts with a brief, sincere "thank you!" At business gatherings, where there might be no hosts, you may seek out the organizers and tell them how successful the event was. At many larger functions, you can slip out without actually saying good-bye to anyone except friends or acquaintances with whom you were most recently speaking.

> *Originality is not everything. The words hosts most want to hear when the evening is over are "Thank you, I had a wonderful time" and "Good night."*
> —JUDITH MARTIN

If you were put on the list of invitees by someone in particular, you might make an effort to thank them for including you.

On the way home, congratulate yourself for being more conversation-savvy than you were several hours ago. If you must remember your faux pas, do so quickly only in order to make a note not to repeat them. But do not dwell on them. Instead, remember the faces that smiled at you and the people who enjoyed talking with you.

CHAPTER 2

How to Be Universally Liked

I have yet to be bored by someone paying me a compliment.
—Otto Van Isch

The single most effective trait you can take into a conversation is the ability to show appreciation. In every conversation, include at least one appreciative remark. If this is something you already do, you might still want to skim this chapter for techniques, useful phrases, and a few do's and don'ts.

In any conversation, business or social, what will make you stand out and be remembered later are the pleasant remarks that show your genuine pleasure at something the other person says, does, or has done. Cultivate this skill, and you will find yourself one of the best-liked individuals at any gathering.

> *To hear how special and wonderful we are is endlessly enthralling.*
> —Gail Sheehy

Conveying Appreciation

Make a habit of watching for something to appreciate in other people. If you work with them, you might already know a few things to mention: "That last report was dynamite." "I noticed your sales figures get better every month." "Love the new phone system."

You might admire people, yet never think to tell them so. You can double your fun and your effectiveness at both work and home by letting people know the pleasant thoughts you have about them.

If you know a person socially, you might know enough to start with: "I drove by your house the other day, and your landscaping is spectacular" or

> *Leaders value other people's worth and opinions and take the time to let them know they are important. It doesn't take very much time to pay someone a compliment. The average is six seconds.*
> —Connie Podesta and Jean Gatz

"I really admire you for finding time to work at the soup kitchen on weekends."

For people you don't know, you'll need to listen carefully to their conversation and find—or make—opportunities to show that you think they're a pretty fine human being.

Don't be embarrassed to say nice things. Our culture more often rewards the snappy put-down (with laughter and renewed contracts for TV sit-coms, for example) than it does the positive remark or the compliment. As long as they are sincerely meant, compliments rarely fail to please.

And don't wait for the big things: "Congratulations on your Nobel Prize!" People get quite enough positive feedback for the big things; it's the little things in life that we are grateful to have someone appreciate: "I enjoy the cartoons you tape on your bulletin board—I always stop for my morning chuckle."

At first, it might feel false to you. Perhaps you're not in the habit of giving compliments easily. But "act as if" this is your style, and soon it will be.

When you can't find anything to appreciate in someone, you can perhaps give them confidence and hope in the future: "We're looking for good things from you in these

> *A gossip is one who talks to you about others; a bore is one who talks to you about himself; and a brilliant conversationalist is one who talks to you about yourself.*
> —Lisa Kirk

next few years." "I can see that you're going to be just what we need around here." "It's going to be a pleasure getting to know you."

Effective Appreciation

- ▶ Is brief. If you go on and on, it's likely to sound fulsome and staged.
- ▶ Is sincere. If you're fabricating something to be appreciative, it will be noticed at some level. Listen to the person's conversation to see what they pride themselves on. That's what you need to appreciate, if you can do so with sincerity. With practice, you will find those issues on

which you can offer sincere compliments. Try to be honestly pleased with the person's accomplishment; this attitude will shine through your words and make them ten times more effective.

> *The deepest principle of Human Nature is the craving to be appreciated.*
> —WILLIAM JAMES

"The art of pleasing consists in being pleased," wrote William Hazlitt. If you cultivate a sense of delight in the achievements of others, you have a successful career and social life ahead of you.

- Is specific. Saying "you're wonderful" is a fraction as meaningful as saying, "That last hire is fabulous. You really know how to pick them!" Or: "I thought that was the most productive meeting we've had in months. I hope you'll chair the next one." Or: "The new rug in the foyer is stunning."

- Is phrased positively rather than negatively. Instead of saying, "I can't believe you did it!" say, "I was so impressed with what you did."

- Makes the other person feel important. The fact that you have remembered an accomplishment makes them feel important in itself. But if you have found something the other person is proud of, and mention it, they will go away thinking nice thoughts about themselves...and you.

- Is sometimes a "transmitted" compliment. When you convey a compliment a third person made, it is very effective: "Jennie tells me she's buying an armoire from you. She says in all her travels she has never seen work as fine as yours."

- Is particularly useful in the workplace. If you want people to give you their best, appreciate their best when you see it. You might also say nice things to them for doing "good" and "better" as well as "best."

- Tells people they are good at what they do. Compliments on people's homes, possessions, clothes, and pets are all welcome, but what people remember are the remarks about what they do well: "You make everyone feel so welcome and spoiled when you entertain." "We've never had anyone at the front desk who gave such a good first impression of the company to visitors."

- Uses verbs like "admire" and "appreciate," and adjectives like "knowledgeable," "memorable," "overwhelming," "remarkable," "satisfying," "stunning," "superb," "valuable."

Appreciative remarks sound something like this:

"All of us have been inspired by the way you won this account."

"Can you stand one more compliment?"

"I admire the way you've bounced back from your accident. I heard the physical therapy you underwent was pretty demanding."

"I admire what you've done with the filing system—we've needed that kind of an overhaul for years."

"I am so impressed with the volunteer work you do—you've really made a difference."

"I couldn't help noticing how beautifully organized your office is—I'd love to keep mine like that, but I can't seem to do it."

"I don't know how I would have managed without your help."

"I especially liked the way you simplified the on-call system."

"I like the way you think!"

"I'm so pleased you made time to come tonight."

"I noticed your rose garden when I drove by the other day—fabulous!"

"I saw your letter to the editor in the paper and was delighted. You said what I'd been thinking except that I wouldn't have been able to word it as well as you did."

> *Nothing makes people so worthy of compliments as occasionally receiving them. One is more delightful for being told one is delightful.*
> —Katherine Fullerton Gerould

"I see you're chairing the fundraising committee again—lucky for us!"

"It must have taken a great deal of courage to call into that radio program—I was hoping someone would object to their rant."

"I've very much enjoyed this conversation."

"I want to tell you how much I appreciate what you're doing for the recycling program in our neighborhood."

"Say, aren't you the one who repotted all the plants in the atrium? It looks 100 percent better!"

"Someone was telling me your workshop was the best we've ever had."

"We're all pleased with the job you're doing."

"What an excellent point! I never thought of it that way."

"You have the knack of knowing what to say during hard times."

"You have the most consistently upbeat attitude—the office would be a gloomy place without you."

> *Everybody likes a compliment.*
> —ABRAHAM LINCOLN

"Your determination is the talk of the neighborhood—we're all grateful that you got them to pave the alley."

"You really know how to make a person feel sensational—thanks for noticing my work."

"Your home is one of a kind—welcoming and functional and gracious."

"Your thoughtfulness after Mother died has stayed with me all this time—thank you again."

"Your window displays are getting phone calls to the store from people passing by—good job!"

"Your work on ethics-in-government legislation has been impressive. I've been waiting years for someone with your combination of skills and energy to come along."

"You've made a unique contribution to my daughter's life."

"You've really got a challenge there—but you seem to be doing well with it."

"You worked hard on that brochure, and it really shows."

Ineffective Appreciation

▶ Exaggerates or is an obvious attempt to flatter: "Here's to the best assistant in the world!" "Our CEO better watch her back now that you're on staff." "You're the greatest pastor we've ever had."

This makes people uncomfortable and will produce the opposite effect of a simple but specific compliment such as: "I can't tell you what a joy it is to me to know that whatever I put on your desk gets done quickly and correctly." "You haven't been here long, but already I'm hearing that you're the one to ask when we need a quick bibliographic search." "Your sermon this morning was inspiring and thought-provoking."

> *An overdose of praise is like ten lumps of sugar in coffee; only a very few people can swallow it.*
> —EMILY POST

Don't express more than you feel. People know when your sentiments are insincere. Use language that feels genuine and comfortable to you.

- Refers to "luck" playing a role in their accomplishments: "Good for you coming up with that slogan—what a stroke of luck!" "I hear you lucked out and got that patent after all." While it is true that luck and timing often play a role in success, it's not gracious—or even truthful—to attribute a person's success to luck instead of to the hard work that must have been involved.

- Is nonspecific: "Hey, great job on the calendar!" "Nice painting!" "You're the best!"

  People would much rather hear details: "This is the first calendar that had photographs you'd actually want to keep afterwards—good choices!" "Your painting takes me back to a summer in Brittany—it's evocative while still leaving room for my own memories." "Your project managed to include everyone's input—a monument to tact and efficiency." It's a little more difficult to elucidate exactly why you like a person's work, but it pays big dividends; their next efforts will be even more praiseworthy.

- Praises the person rather than the action or the deed: "You're a fantastic pianist!" "You're a terrific host!" "You're a top-notch manager."

  Instead, say something like: "You played that last piece with such exquisite feeling that I could almost smell the sea." "You always make me feel so welcome—I love being invited here!" "I hear nothing but good things from your division—you have evidently found the right balance between benign leadership and high expectations."

  If you tell someone they are an extraordinary chef, they reject it; they know there are hundreds of chefs better than they are. However, tell them that you could eat their shepherd's pie three times a day and they think that, just possibly, you might have a point. A great chef, probably not. Successful at the shepherd's pie, possibly yes. And so they accept the compliment and will feed you better than ever the next time.

- Is patronizing. When a remark seems to be evaluating or judging or giving someone a grade, it doesn't feel like a real compliment: "Well, look at you! Who would have thought you'd graduate magna cum laude." "That was good of you, to give money to that homeless woman." "You bought a car all by yourself? Good going."

Accepting Appreciation

When you're on the receiving end of an appreciative comment, acknowledge it with a simple expression of pleasure. Your goal is to further the goodwill that was begun with the other person's comment, to reflect back the kindness and pleasure.

Don't parrot back their compliment: "I like your dress, too." "Your presentation was excellent, too." "You played well, too." If you mean such a remark, put a little spin on it: "I can't believe it! I was about to tell you the same thing! Great minds and all that...." "You beat me to the punch. I was just going to mention *your* report."

Too many people, in the interests of false modesty, respond to a compliment by repudiating it: "Oh, heavens, it was nothing." "I wrote that report in five minutes, and I didn't think it was very good." "This old jacket? I've had it forever." "Thanks, but it really wasn't that big of a deal." "It was pure luck." Brushing off the compliment says to the other person that they don't really know what they're talking about.

If you feel compelled to share the credit, at least wait a few sentences to let the person enjoy giving you a compliment. Then you could add: "You know, I couldn't have done it without the staff."

A compliment is a gift, not to be thrown away carelessly unless you want to hurt the giver.
—Eleanor Hamilton

The easiest comeback to a compliment is a simple, "How kind of you!" This reflects the cordiality onto the other person and is, in fact, an appreciative remark in itself.

Respond to a compliment with something like:

"Aren't you nice to tell me that."

"Hey! You noticed! Thanks!"

"How kind of you!"

"How nice of you to say so."

"I appreciate the complimentary words."

"I appreciate the positive feedback."

"I appreciate your concern."

"I appreciate your noticing."

"I like to hear that."

"I'm glad it turned out as well as it did."
"I'm happy that you're pleased."
"I'm so happy you told me."
"It was an exciting project to work on."
"I've heard a lot about you, too—all of it good!"
"Thank you."
"Thanks for mentioning it."
"Thanks. Frank speaks highly of you too."
"That's so nice of you to tell me."
"You remembered!"
"Your interest is a delight—thanks."

CHAPTER 3

How to Listen Successfully

> *Research has consistently demonstrated that ineffective listening habits present the most common barriers to success in relationships and careers.*
>
> —Larry Barker and Kittie Watson

Most of us take for granted the simple verb *listen*, but its dictionary definition might surprise us. *The American Heritage Dictionary* says to listen means "to make an effort to hear something" and "to pay attention; heed." If you want to be a good conversationalist, remember that listening is more than simply letting another person talk. We're asked to pay attention, to make an effort, to heed.

Listening is thus an active, not a passive, behavior consisting of hearing, understanding, and remembering.

A good listener takes part in the conversation, offering ideas and questions to keep the talk flowing. You want to say enough to add something new, but not so much that you overshadow the other person. Good conversation is a balancing act, a teeter-totter, a turn-taking endeavor.

Englishman Raymond Mortimer once observed that in the United States, conversation "is not tennis, in

> *It is not enough to remain silent while others are talking; that is not listening in any true sense. One must be manifestly attentive to the speaker, asking an occasional question, commenting upon what has been said. The good listener brings out the best in people. He is responsive. His eyes light up occasionally with interest and pleasure. Not for an instant does he permit his attention to wander.*
>
> —Lillian Eichler

which you return the other fellow's service, but golf, in which you go on hitting your own ball."

In the same way that you don't want to play conversational golf yourself, you don't want to leave the other person hitting their own ball all the time. Listening means playing tennis, where you return the ball. And, like a good game of tennis, you want to see that you're well matched, that you're both playing with the same ball, and that you alternate turns hitting it.

> *Anybody can hear—it takes brains to listen.*
> —JOANNE GREENBERG

If you think back over meetings, conferences, visits with friends, and other conversations, you will perhaps recall that a great deal of time could have been saved if everyone had listened the first time. How many times did questions have to be answered again, or information repeated, or incidents retold? Not listening costs us time and energy—to say nothing of the disappointed looks on the faces of those who'd already told us that very thing.

What Makes a Good Listener?

- You focus on the other person, not allowing yourself to be distracted by what is going on around you or by your own thoughts and concerns.
- You not only listen, but you *show* you are listening by appearing highly interested, leaning slightly forward, nodding occasionally, and saying "uh-huh" at intervals.
- Dale Carnegie advised people, "To be interesting, be interested." Try to find some aspect of the other person's talk that genuinely interests you.
- You make and maintain eye contact, occasionally breaking it so that the other person doesn't feel as though they're under a microscope.
- You subtly mirror the other person: smile, frown, nod, and laugh when they do.

> *I happen to disagree with the well-entrenched theory that the art of conversation is merely the art of being a good listener. Such advice invites people to be cynical with one another and full of fake; when a conversation becomes a monologue, poked along with tiny cattle-prod questions, it isn't a conversation any more. It is a strained, manipulative game, tiring and perhaps even lonely.*
> —BARBARA WALTERS

- ▶ You ask pertinent questions that show you're following the other person's train of thought.
- ▶ To listen effectively, you need to not only hear what the other person is saying but to understand it. This means you also ask clarifying questions. To be called a conversation, there needs to be some back-and-forthing. Therefore, you will want to insert some of your own thoughts on the subject. Try sentences like:

"Along those same lines, do you…"

"Am I hearing this right? You think…"

"And do you know what are your competitors are up to?"

"Can you give me an example?"

"Can you go back a minute to this business about the ferret?"

"Did you see the op-ed piece in the paper yesterday about that?"

"From your perspective, you're saying it's a bust."

"Hmm, but if that happened every time…"

"How did you get from there to here?"

> *If you want to be listened to, you should put in time listening.*
> —MARGE PIERCY

"How do you feel about the new products in that line?"

"How were you able to manage with one arm in a cast?"

"I agree with you about the fault line, but what about quakes under 3.0?"

"I can see why this is so important to you."

"If I understand you correctly, you believe…"

"I hadn't thought of it that way."

"I read an article about that last week, but I didn't understand how it's superior to what's already out there."

"I see what you mean, but does it always work out like that?"

"I think I see where you're going with this, but keep talking."

"I thought of you when I heard about the latest hybrid."

"In other words…?"

"I've always wanted to ask someone how that works."

"Let me see if I get where you're coming from."

"Now that's intriguing—tell me more."

"On the other hand, what if nobody shows up?"

"Say, you'd probably be interested in a little company just starting up."

"So, in essence, you think...?"

"So what do you think will happen next?"

"So what you're saying is...?"

"So would you say that all synthetic vinyls will react like that?"

"So you're suggesting that..."

"Tell me more about the silver mine you mentioned earlier."

"That must have been a rough year for your family."

"That's a new way of looking at it."

> Exclusive attention to the person who is speaking to you is very important. Nothing else is so flattering as that.
> —CHARLES W. ELIOT

"That's really an accomplishment—whatever possessed you?"

"Wait a minute, what's 'linuron'?"

"Well, but then, what happens if...?"

"What are the disadvantages?"

"What do you mean by 'soon'?"

"What got you started in this direction?"

"What happened then?"

"When you mentioned soy candles just now, I remembered that you used them for a school fundraiser a few years ago."

"When you say 'jazz,' what artists are you talking about?"

"When you talk about flaws, what do you mean?"

"Where could I find more information about that?"

"Will you be able to reproduce those results?"

"Would I be able to get in on that?"

"Would you do the same thing again?"

"You sound absolutely sold on it!"

"You're really serious about this, aren't you?"

> A good listener is not only popular everywhere, but after a while he knows something.
> —WILSON MIZNER

- ▶ You repeat or summarize the other person's key points, not in a parrotlike manner, but rewording them somewhat.
- ▶ You leave a little pause after the other person's words in case they have something to add. Too many listeners take the first chance to rush into speech themselves.
- ▶ You refer back to things said earlier in the conversation to show that you heard what was said.
- ▶ You are patient. If the other person searches for a word or speaks haltingly or pauses, you allow them time to complete their thoughts.
- ▶ You try to identify with the speaker, putting yourself in their place, feeling what they're feeling. If nothing else, mentally relate the other person's experiences to your own.
- ▶ Above all, you cultivate an attitude of wanting to listen. The better you become at listening, the more clearly you'll appreciate its benefits, and you will end up wanting to listen. But in the beginning, act as if you want to listen. Your attentiveness will show.

What Makes a Poor Listener?

- ▶ Your attention wanders to a problem at home or work, and you lose the thread of what the other person is saying.
- ▶ You are busy thinking of what you're going to say next, waiting for your turn to speak.
- ▶ You rarely look the other person in the eye.
- ▶ You can't seem to help showing that you're bored: you look at your watch, shuffle your feet, check out the rest of the room.
- ▶ At the first opportunity, you grab the conversational ball and run with it, even if it means interrupting the other person. You'd much rather talk than listen.
- ▶ You constantly finish the other person's sentences. This is insulting, patronizing, and irritating.
- ▶ You really aren't interested in the other person's topic, so you change the subject.

> *Isn't it boring...how people always want to tell you their own stories instead of listening to yours? I suppose that's why psychiatrists are better than friends; the paid listener doesn't interrupt with his own experiences.*
> —HELEN VAN SLYKE

- You ask so many questions that the other person feels harried, grilled, and breathless. Many of your questions are about hair-splitting details that really don't matter,

- You're busy judging the other person: she just said "between you and I"; his pants sure are wrinkled; she's got an awfully high voice; he doesn't seem like the sharpest knife in the drawer. This negative attitude is often picked up by the other person. They're not sure what's going on, but they think perhaps they won't spend much time with you.

- You like to one-up the other person. If they've read a good book, you've read two. If they attended a professional football game, you've got season tickets.

- If you're in an office setting, you tend to multitask while conversing with someone. This way you get two things done at once, you think, as you file reports, stack up the outgoing mail, and log off your computer.

> *Almost any business situation will be handled differently, and with different results, by someone who is listening and someone who isn't.*
> —MARK H. McCORMACK

- You rush the other person, giving the impression that they are taking far too much of your time: "Yeah, you already mentioned that. So what did you have to pay finally?"

- You are completely silent. You figure listening means shutting up, whereas the other person would appreciate hearing a word or two from you.

CHAPTER 4

How to Keep a Conversation Going—or Stop One

> *Humans abhor a vacuum. The immediate filling of a vacuum is one of the basic functions of speech. Meaningless conversations are no less important in our lives than meaningful ones.*
> —LIDIA GINZBURG

You've probably already discovered that in most conversations, you need a few "empty" words and phrases that (1) indicate to the other person you're listening attentively, or (2) encourage the other person to keep talking, or (3) fill in that little expectant pause some people leave for you.

Sometimes being silent is appropriate, but it's helpful to have a handful of conversational fillers in your armamentarium. People generally don't pay too much attention to these soothing little rejoinders, so it's not what you say as much as that you respond with something.

Without stopping the flow of the conversation with more substantive remarks, these interjections let the other person know you're interested and involved.

Don't worry about the essential inanity of these words and phrases. Like a film score, your words provide a background for the other person's talk without calling attention to themselves. These responses are a fairly standard part of contemporary culture, and they fill a need to give conversations the appearance of being two-sided. The problem arises when you use the same word or phrase for everything ("Awesome!" "Oh, yeah, awesome!" "Wow, awesome!"), at which point the expression becomes an annoying verbal tic (see Chapter 8).

Vary your responses and use a lowered tone so as not to call attention to your rejoinders.

You probably already use some such phrases, but you might like to collect a few new ones. Choose those that suit your personality and that you can say with some sincerity.

To show that you're listening, say something like:

"Absolutely!"

"Aha!"

"All right!"

"Amazing!"

"And so then...?"

"And then...?"

"Are you serious?"

"Awesome!"

"Darn!"

"For instance...?"

"Gee."

"Good grief!"

"Gosh."

"Hard to believe!"

"Hmm."

"How interesting."

"I agree."

"I didn't know that."

"I'd never thought of it like that."

"I don't believe it!"

"I hear you."

"I'll bet you're really excited about this."

"I'll say."

"Incredible."

"I see."

"I see that."

"I see what you mean."

"Isn't that something!"

"No kidding!"

"No, really?"

"Oh?"

"Oh dear."

"Really!"

"Really?"

"Right."

"Seriously?"

"Sure!"

"That makes sense."

"That must've been difficult."

"That's a good point."

"That's a novel way of doing it."

"That's egregious!"

[Thumbs up]

"Too bad!"

"Well, who knew?"

"What an accomplishment!"

"What do you know about that!"

"Wow."

"Yes, yes."

"You bet!"

"You can say that again!"

"You can't be serious."

"You couldn't be more right."

"You don't say!"

"You mean...?"

"You're kidding!"

> *Listening, not imitation, may be the sincerest form of flattery.*
> —JOYCE BROTHERS

To encourage the other person to continue, say something like:

"And?"
"And then what?"
"Can you tell me more?"
"Continue. This is great."
"Could you give me an example?"
"Did they really?"
"Do you mean that...?"
"For instance?"
"Give me an example."
"Go on."
"How interesting."
"I'd like to learn more about that."
"I hadn't thought of it that way."
"I know very little about this."
"I like what you're saying."
"Is there a downside?"
"It's hard to believe."
"I wish I'd known that before."
"Keep talking—this is great information."
"No, no, keep going."
"No, really?'
"Not really!"
"Oh?"
"So then...?"
"Tell me more."
"That must have been tough on you."
"That's a new way of looking at it."
"That's intriguing."
"That's news to me."

> *Good listeners are perceived as good conversationalists.*
> —Susan RoAne

"That's really interesting."

"This is the first time I've understood that—please continue."

"What a shock."

"What do you mean by that?"

"What problems have you run into?"

"You can say that again!"

"You mean…?"

"You mean that?"

"You're saying that…?"

"You've really studied this, haven't you?"

To fill in the pause that some people leave for your "half" of the conversation, say something like:

"Amazing."

"Fascinating!"

"Good grief!"

"Good point."

"I agree."

"I didn't know that."

"I hear you."

"I'll say."

"I see."

"I see where you're going with this."

"Life is interesting."

"No, really?"

"Of course!"

"Oh dear."

"Oh, yes, absolutely."

"Really!"

"Right. Right."

"Sure enough."

"That must've been wild."

> *Silences have a climax, when you have got to speak.*
> —ELIZABETH BOWEN

"What a deal."

"What a story."

"Who'd believe it!"

"Wow."

"You're absolutely right."

"You're darn right."

You don't want to use the above words and phrases with someone who is delivering a monologue in your presence; it will only encourage them to continue. Instead, fill that space (if you are lucky enough to get one) with a subtle, polite signal that you aren't all that fascinated by what the other person is saying. Sometimes people climb on hobby horses and forget to dismount. We must help them.

If you want to trot the other person in the direction of winding down the conversation or at least allowing you to talk, try something like:

[Being quiet]

"Hmm [in a monotone]."

"I just remembered something that will interest you."

"I thought of you when I heard..."

"I've always wanted to ask you..."

"Oh."

"Really [flatly]."

"Say, I read an article the other day about that."

[Small, ambiguous, detached grunt]

"That reminds me..."

"That's a great point, but you know what occurs to me?"

"Uh-huh [patently patient]."

"Well, that was quite a story."

"Well, what do you know about that!"

"Yes, well, that's quite a thing."

"You must be glad that's over."

> She will not be interrupted. Break into her train of thought, and she simply starts over. From the top. It is like trying to hold a conversation with a cassette.
> —SHANA ALEXANDER

Henry S. Haskins once advised, "The time to stop talking is when the other person nods his head affirmatively but says nothing." This is an excellent strategy for you in a case like this. After a few nods accompanied by silence, most people will take your hint.

Be tactful, however. The other person is there as a friend, colleague, or duly invited guest, so you won't want to be noticeably rude. As Robert Lynd put it, "A man may forgive many wrongs, but he cannot easily forgive anyone who makes it plain that his conversation is tedious."

In the event that the other person is riding a stampeding horse and cannot be halted, you will have to use a more aggressive approach:

> *Make sure you have finished speaking before your audience has finished listening.*
> —Dorothy Sarnoff

"Do you have the time? Oops, I need to make a phone call."

"Excuse me. I need to take care of my contact lens."

"I mustn't monopolize your attention. Enjoy the rest of the evening."

"I promised to help Julie with the refreshments—will you excuse me?"

"I think I'm coming down with a sore throat. I need to get something to drink."

"It's been grand talking with you."

"Mother always told me to mingle at these things, so I'd better go do my duty."

"The food looks terrific—I think I'll get a plate while it's still warm."

(See Chapter 1 for more so-long-it's-been-good-to-know-you lines.)

CHAPTER 5

How to Ask and Answer Questions

When you know how to ask the right questions, you can talk to anyone about anything.
—Dorothy Leeds

A basic staple of conversation, questions allow you to find out about other people, to keep a conversation going, and to show your interest in what people are saying. They can also buy you time, clarify what you don't understand, and demonstrate your openness and curiosity.

Where a statement might provoke resistance ("I didn't like the idea"), a question ("What did you think about that idea?") will stimulate thought, prolong the discussion, and convey appreciation of the other person's input.

Adding humor to a question signifies that you aren't being aggressive and that if the person wants to evade the question, they can also use humor.

The impulse to ask questions is among the more primitive human lusts.
—Rose Macaulay

Questions are either (1) open-ended, which elicit a complex answer, or (2) close-ended, which elicit a one-word answer, often *yes* or *no*.

Open-ended questions start with *who, when, what, why, where,* or *how.* Close-ended questions generally start with "Do you...," "Did you...," "Are you...," "Have you...." The close-ended question extracts a small piece of information but tends to bring the conversation to a stop.

Some people can take a close-ended question and elaborate on it for quite a long time. Others—those who are literal minded—will give you a one-word answer. Period. The end. Now what?

You can use close-ended questions to speed up a conversation in which you are simply seeking information, to indicate subtly your lack of interest in the conversation, or even as a way of signaling good-bye: "Are you leaving soon?"

The first example of each pair below is close-ended, the second open-ended:

Do you like your new office?" (Yes/No)
"How did you manage to get a better office?"

"Are you moving to Seattle?" (Yes/No)
"How do you feel about it?"

"Did you enjoy Paris?" (Yes/No)
"What did you like most about Paris?"

"Is that hard to learn?" (Yes/No)
"How would I go about learning that?"

"Do you like your work?" (Yes/No)
"How did you get interested in that field?"

"Is life treating you well?" (Yes/No)
"How are you coming along with the house remodeling?"

"Is that a new process?" (Yes/No)
"Will you explain that to me?"

"Do you live in the area?" (Yes/No)
"What brought you to this area?"

"Are you a reader?" (Yes/No)
"What have you been reading lately?"

"Do you like the firm?" (Yes/No)
"What do you like about the firm?"

"Do you golf?" (Yes/No)

"What do you think about golf?"

If it's time for you to ask a question, but you don't have one, think of the other person's last topic and ask who (who won that event this year?), what (what did your boss think?), when (when is your team playing next?), where (where could I find one of those?), or how (how did you find out?).

> *The impulse to answer a question—any question—is as automatic as the "fight or flight" response. Everyone, including that rare individual who refuses to answer, pays more attention to a question than to a statement.*
> —Dorothy Leeds

To avoid the appearance of interviewing someone, you can replace questions with statements that do the same job: "Tell me how you got into this business." "Explain how you did that." "Take me through a typical day." "Describe it for me."

When misused or overused, questions are annoying. Asking too many questions makes other people feel positively hunted and is often the fallback position of a poor conversationalist; questions substitute for thought, for self-revelation, for genuine exchanges.

Overall, in any conversation, balance questions with statements. All questions or all statements do not produce a good back-and-forth exchange.

Don't answer your own questions! Some people ask a question and then rush to answer it.

And don't ask a question if you don't really want an honest answer: "What should I do about it?" "What did you think about my suggestion at the meeting?" "Would you keep my dog for a couple of days while I'm out of town?"

Bad Questions

- Are judgmental or aggressive.

    "Are you going to eat the whole thing?"

    "Are you one of those environmentalists?"

    "Didn't you realize it was a mistake?"

    "Didn't you see the warning sign?"

    "Did you ever consider dying your hair?"

    "Do you always talk so fast?"

"Do you understand what I just said?"

"Have you thought about going on a diet?"

"How can you say such a thing?"

"How many times have I told you it won't work?"

"Is this all there is?"

"Weren't you paying attention?"

"What did you do that for?"

"What did you think would happen?"

"Whatever made you think I'd want one?"

"Who did you think was going to pay for it?"

"You're not leaving before you finished, are you?"

> *A self-taught conversationalist, his style with new acquaintances had the immediate warmth of an investigative journalist tracking down discrepancies in a municipal budget.*
> —Mary Kay Blakely

▶ Are intrusive.

"Are those hair implants?"

"Do you make quite a bit at what you do?"

"Haven't you lost an awful lot of weight lately?"

"Have you had a face lift?"

"How are you going to vote next month?"

"How much did you pay for this house?"

"How much of a raise did you get this year?"

"Just between us, have you ever taken Viagra?"

"What did you pay for your dress?"

"When did you start dying your hair?"

"Why don't you have children?"

▶ Are numerous. Delivered one after another, they make the other person feel attacked. Often this rapid-fire and unrelenting questioning is more of a nervous tic, as if the person is asking because they don't know what else to do and as if the answer doesn't really matter.

"Did you say two rabbits or three?"

"What kind of rabbits?"

"Why rabbits?"

"What color were they?"

"Did they notice the fox?"

"Is that it, that's the joke?"

It's often true that people who go in for this kind of questioning fail to listen to the answers. If you are the questioner type, try listening more carefully to the other person's answer. That will slow down your questions as well as let the person see that your questions really do have a point and that you care about the answers.

> *Just as you shouldn't be a monologuist, neither should you be an interrogator. There will not be a quiz after the evening is over.*
> —LARRY KING

▶ Are too broad. This type of question is sometimes welcome. But where "conversation lite" is the norm, there's rarely time to get into a meaty topic.

"So. What do you think about poverty?"

"The Big Bang Theory—do you believe in it?"

"What do you know about global warming?"

"What's wrong with kids today?"

▶ Sometimes begin with *why*. These questions — although often quite good—can, at other times, be accusatory, aggressive, or overly personal. *Why* questions put people on the defensive. They feel obliged to explain their reasoning, motives, and actions. If you ask "What happened...?" instead of "Why...?" the person can relate the facts in an objective manner.

> *She had the habit into which your poor conversationalists usually fall, namely, asking questions. I know nothing more disagreeable than to be subjected to the society of a questioner.*
> —SARAH J. HALE

"Why are you going to a place like that?"

"Why can't you make your own?"

"Why didn't you do that?"

"Why didn't you just pick up the phone and call?"

"Why did you do that?"

"Why did you think it would run?"

"Why do you always do that?"

"Why do you need that book?"
"Why on earth did you buy it in the first place?"
"Why would you ask that?"
"Why would you buy two of them?"
"Why would you do such a thing?"
"Why would you think I'd say yes?"

Good Questions

- Relate to what the other person has just said.
  "Did they ever find out who was responsible?"
  "Did you ever go back there?"
  "Do you know if it would grow in a Zone 5?"
  "Is she still hospitalized?"
  "Why do you think the vote went that way?"
  "Would you recommend them?"
- Help you find common ground.
  "Do you live in this neighborhood?"
  "Have you worked here long?"
  "How do you know our hosts?"
  "What brings you here tonight?"
  "What is your interest in this topic?"
  "When did you join?"
- Move the conversation along.
  "Along those same lines, would a generator do the trick?"
  "And then...?"
  "Are you saying that anyone can do it?"
  "Can you give me an example?"
  "Do you mean she advocates the same thing for all children?"
  "How did you arrive at that conclusion?"
  "So who finally won?"
  "What happened then?"
  "What kind of side effects are there?"

- Lead to complex answers.

    "Do you know anything about the new security regulations at the airport?"

    "I see you have hummingbirds in your yard. How did you attract them?"

    "What brought you to Des Moines?"

    "What colleges is your son looking at?"

    "Where would you live if you could live anywhere in the world?"

    "You've been to Cairo. How would I find a good hotel there?"

- Are sensitive.

    "Excuse me for asking, but..."

    "I'd love to know, if you don't mind telling me..."

    "If you don't mind my asking..."

    "I hope I'm not being too personal, but..."

    "Please feel free not to answer, but..."

> *She was the kind of woman who liked to ask questions to which she already knew the answers. It gave her a sense of security.*
> —MARGARET MILLAR

- Are neutral.

    "Do you know if our water rates have gone up lately?"

    "I saw you admiring the roses. Are you a gardener yourself?"

    "Is the public library still open on weekends, do you know?"

    "Say, do you know what kind of a tree that is?"

    "We have visitors coming next month. Is there a local hotel you would recommend?"

- Are concrete. "You think so?" and "Is that right?" aren't really questions. Concrete questions use words that the other person has used, and builds on them. They tell the person you are interested in their topic. If you've been discussing constructing a rock wall, ask specific questions:

    "Have you found a good book on rock walls?"

    "How long do you expect it to take you?"

    "What kind of rocks will you use?"

    "Where are you buying your rocks?"

    "Would a person need help, or can one person handle it?"

If you're interested in what the other person is saying, this sort of question will come naturally. When you're not interested, but want to continue the conversation, you might have to work at finding good concrete questions.

In general, concrete questions sound something like:

"I agree with you about the benefits of walking, but do you think twenty minutes three times a week is enough?"

"I'm not familiar with your company. Can you tell me about it?"

"I understand you write the music for several television reality shows. How did you get into that line of work?"

"I've always wanted to ask you how you sold your first painting."

"What do you think about hybrid cars?"

"What do you think will happen next?"

"What would happen if television advertising were banned from children's programming?"

Responding to Bad Questions

You are never obliged to answer a question. If someone poses a question to you that is aggressive, intrusive, or rude, there are several responses you can try aside from simple silence, a blank stare, or excusing yourself and moving away.

> *It has always puzzled me, in my business, that people think they have to answer questions, no matter how disagreeable or dangerous, just because they were asked. Of course, we journalists would be out of business if they didn't.*
>
> —JUDITH MARTIN

"Do you mind telling me why you are asking?"

"Do you need to know?"

"Excuse me, but that's personal with me."

"How much did we pay for the house? Enough."

"I don't really talk about it."

"I'm not sure what you're getting at."

"I'm sorry, did you ask me if…?"

"I'm sorry, that's not the sort of information I give out."

"I'm surprised you're asking."

"I never discuss that in any month that has an 'r' in it. Or that doesn't have an 'r' in it."

"May we change the subject?"

"My salary? It's about what you'd expect."

"Only my hairdresser knows for sure."

"Ouch!"

[Silence]

"That's pretty personal, isn't it?"

"This is a first. People usually don't ask questions like that."

"What do you mean?"

"Why do you ask?"

"Why do you want to know?"

"Would you mind saying that again?"

CHAPTER 6

How and When to Tell Jokes

I had thought, on starting this composition, that I should define what humor means to me. However, every time I tried to, I had to go and lie down with a cold wet cloth on my head.
—Dorothy Parker

What is funny? The short answer is: Who knows? The joke that triggers a burst of laughter from one listener might be met with a puzzled look from another.

In general, steer clear of jokes at any business or social gathering where there are more than two people in your conversational group. If there are only two people—and they consist of you and your best friend—go ahead and tell it.

Admittedly, a few people possess an impeccable sense of timing, appropriateness, brevity, and joke delivery. You are probably not—statistically speaking—one of them.

You might be quite funny and have a bottomless fund of great jokes. But there's a place for jokes—during halftime, over dinner with family, hiking with friends—and business or social affairs with colleagues and acquaintances are not it. It takes a whole other level of joke savvy to insert a joke into the slightly ritualized conversation of non-intimates.

It is a difficult thing to like anybody else's ideas of being funny.
—Gertrude Stein

Aside from saving you the embarrassment of a joke that falls flat, there's a bigger problem. Jokes aren't really conversation. Although a well-placed joke can set off a discussion, provide lightness when needed, or illuminate a subject, a joke is a way of talking at people, not with them. Joke-telling puts you on a different level than the people you're with, even if for only a moment.

Ask yourself why you want to tell a joke.

(a) You feel that you should say something and you can't think of anything else.

(b) There's an awkward pause, and no one else seems prepared to fill it.

(c) You're tired of So-and-So being the center of attention.

(d) You feel it's about your turn to have the floor

(e) It fits in perfectly with what the last person said, and spins the conversation in a new direction

> *Jokes have a tendency to be used when people are desperate for something to say. They stop conversation, not encourage it.*
> —ANNE BABER AND LYNNE WAYMON

The only acceptable answer is (e).

More useful than a joke is the one-liner that relates closely to what is being said. Unlike most jokes, the one-liner doesn't stop the conversation. It keeps it going in the same direction.

A: "The worst part of our moth infestation is that little dusty spot they leave behind when you kill them."

B: "Sounds as though you need some mothwash."

A: "Does anyone else react poorly to coffee? I get headaches and my eyes hurt."

B: "Maybe before drinking your coffee, you should take the spoon out of the cup."

A: "We went to the ballet last night, and I'm still marveling at the way they dance on their toes."

B: "Why don't they just get taller dancers?"

A: "And I found three more fabulous seashells for my collection."

B. "I have a seashell collection, too, except that I keep mine scattered on beaches all over the world."

A: "Yes, we're definitely getting married although I haven't picked a date yet."

B: "What? You're bringing a date to your own wedding?"

A: "We're working on a building on South Main. It's going to provide office space solely for ophthalmologists and opticians."

B: "A site for sore eyes, eh?"

Unfortunately, you have to either have an armload of versatile one-liners or be as quick-witted as a badger to use this tactic. And when it is overused, it is more deadly than a bad joke. A conversation with you in it would have the hiccups.

> *Wit is the salt of conversation, not the food, and few things in the world are more wearying than a sarcastic attitude towards life.*
> —AGNES REPPLIER

If you must tell a joke—because you are good at it and because the joke fits perfectly into the conversation—you will be most successful if you:

- ▶ Key the joke to something just said, so that it follows from the conversation. It doesn't matter how funny the joke is. If it has nothing to do with the topic under discussion, don't tell it.
- ▶ Know your audience and match the joke to the group, the event, or the surroundings.
- ▶ Don't telegraph your expectations. Have you ever felt your smile grow forced when someone says:

"Have I got a joke for you!"

"I can top that."

"If you think that's funny, listen to this."

"Listen, I heard the funniest joke today."

"Oh, hey, you've got to hear this joke."

"Oh my gosh, when I heard this joke, I laughed so hard."

"Oh, this is so funny!"

"This joke is hysterical."

"You're going to die—listen to this."

"You're going to love this joke."

"You've probably already heard this, but it's so funny I know you won't mind."

Advance advertising is not what's meant by "warming up the crowd." Instead, it notifies people that you expect them to double up with laughter. And that makes them tense. Maybe they will howl at your punch line, but they would have enjoyed it more if you hadn't let a little air out of the balloon first.

The best jokes slip into the conversation so that by the time listeners realize a joke is in progress, the punch line is being delivered—to their surprise and delight.

There might not be anyone left who follows a joke with, "But seriously, folks..." However, if there is, and if it's you, drop it. It's old. And it's not funny.

- If it's a long joke, it had better be really, really funny and really, really appropriate. You should have enjoyed previous success with the joke in order to be sure it's both.

> *The announcement that you are going to tell a good story (and the chuckle that precedes it) is always a dangerous opening.*
> —MARGOT ASQUITH

- Jokes don't translate well when you're in a group with mixed backgrounds: those whose first language is not English, those who might not understand jargon or an "in" term, young people who wouldn't catch a reference to some bit of culture familiar to older people—and vice versa.

- Stay away from off-color jokes. Unless you're telling it to dear friends, an off-color joke doesn't do you any good. No matter how hard your audience laughs or how much it seems to appreciate your humor, you will be pigeonholed as someone not quite top drawer.

- Avoid sexist, ethnic, and religious targets, even if you are a member of that group yourself or even if "some of your best friends" are or even if it happens to be a very funny joke. It's not worth it.

- Never joke about another person in the group—about their name, habits, hometown, profession, appearance, or past. It's not a question of whether the joke is upbeat or benign or appropriate. No one enjoys being singled out this way. When you are the subject of the joke, the laughter doesn't feel good no matter how

> *It's no longer socially acceptable to make bigoted statements and racist remarks. Some people are having an awful time with that: "I didn't know anybody would be offended!" Well, where have you been? I remember when people got away with it and they don't anymore.*
> —JUDITH MARTIN

58 *The Art of Talking to Anyone*

vigorously you tell yourself they're not laughing at you. Because that's what it feels like.

▶ Puns are a special problem. Unless you are with people who like puns, and you're all throwing some on the table, save them for a punpal. Michael Iapoce, in *A Funny Thing Happened on the Way to the Boardroom*, says it best: "As you may well know, puns and word plays will most often elicit a groan. If there is laughter, it is given up grudgingly. This is because, by its very nature, a pun is a statement of how clever one is—how much more clever than the audience. The speaker is in effect saying, 'Look at me, I thought of this cute word play, aren't I smart?'"

▶ If you have any doubts about the joke, err on the side of caution. In a social situation, there's nothing as painful as a joke people have to pretend to enjoy.

▶ One joke is a good limit to set yourself. Telling more is perceived as grandstanding. Not even if they beg you. "Leave them wanting more" applies here.

So you've told your joke. What do you say if you realize your joke offended someone?

Apologize as briefly and as sincerely as you can, and hope that someone changes the subject. Try saying:

"If it's any consolation, I've learned a good lesson."

"I'm sorry. I should have known better."

"I'm sorry. I wasn't thinking."

"I was trying to be funny, but it was inappropriate."

What do you do if people don't get your joke or don't appear to find it as funny as you do?

First, do not retell it, only louder this time, hoping the point will register. Second, don't try to jolly people into getting it ("Come on, think about it for a minute").

People do not like people whose jokes they don't understand. They feel stupid and need to blame someone. If you want to leave with

> "Ha-ha," said Sir Mark. "Hum. Very good, yes, ha-ha!" Thumbs under his lapels he looked, however, rather anxiously round the room. Conversation with someone at whose joke you have heartily laughed without seeing the point is apt to become precarious.
>
> —Elizabeth Bowen

How and When to Tell Jokes 59

the goodwill of your listeners, say something to make them feel less dim-witted. (And consider the possibility that you shouldn't be telling jokes away from home.) You could say:

"I don't know why I tell jokes when I'm so poor at it."

"I'm sorry. I think I told that wrong. My brother's going to have to explain it to me."

"I need to retire that joke. This is the second time I've fallen flat on my face with it."

The world needs laughter, and good humor is a success wherever it goes, so this caveat about joke-telling is not meant to dampen high spirits or to make a case for sedate conversation. The point is rather to remember that conversation is a dialogue, and some jokesters forget that. If you're a gifted storyteller and you know people love your jokes (and they're brief and appropriate), go for it. We need your kind. The rest of us will save our jokes for family and close friends.

CHAPTER 7

How to Deal With Conversational Predicaments

If you've made a social blunder, confess and apologize, hoping for graciousness, and then shut up. Don't spend the rest of the night describing what you did, trying to wear out the guilt of it by public contrition.

—BARBARA WALTERS

Those "oops!" moments in conversations can be caused by you or by someone else, but whoever trips on the rug is going to need a hand up. Knowing the right thing to say in these situations will make you more confident about the occasional slip-up.

You Forget Someone's Name

This is such a common occurrence that most people—even people whose name you really, really ought to know—will forgive you. But you will feel terrible about it and will want to say something.

You can sometimes save yourself by avoiding their name: "Oh, hey, it's you!" "It's good to see you again." "How long has it been?" "You're looking good!" "Hello! How are you? Have you seen the smorgasbord?"

If you socialize much or attend many meetings, however, you will probably have to devise a system to win the name game:

- ▶ Use the person's name several times right after being introduced to them and while looking at their face. Hope that the connection sticks.
- ▶ Associate the name and face in some way (Bonnie is a bonny young woman; Jay looks vaguely like Jay Leno; Mary is going to marry that fellow who works in Production—what the heck is his name?).

- ► As soon as possible after meeting the person, jot their name and several keywords about them in a notebook.
- ► Ask for the person's business card and once you get home, note a few pertinent words about the person on the card.
- ► Pay attention. Often the reason a name escapes us is that we're distracted, or we weren't listening carefully when we first heard it.

Unfortunately, the worst cases of forgotten-name syndrome occur when you have known the person for a long time and you know their name as well as your own, but you can't seem to bring it up on your mental screen. As a first resort, try not to indicate that their name escapes you. But if it becomes apparent, without dwelling overmuch on it, say something like:

"Go ahead, I owe you—forget *my* name!"

"Has this ever happened to you? Tell me it has!"

"Help! I've gone blank."

"I know your name as well as my own—you know I do! I wonder if stress causes this?"

"I must have filed it in my right brain, and I'm in my left brain at the moment."

"I must have some corrupted files in my brain."

"It's been that kind of a day."

"Mother told me there would be days like this."

"Tell me you once forgot the name of a very nice person."

But please, if you want to appear intelligent and hip, do not use the badly overused and inane "I'm having a senior moment."

If someone forgets your name, be gracious. Be glad you didn't forget theirs.

You Hurt or Insult Someone

You were joking when you told someone her dress made her look like a streetwalker, when you told another he was dumber than a box of rocks, and when you asked your host if the Salvation Army sent a decorator along with their furniture. Unfortunately, they didn't think you were joking.

You've overstepped the bounds of good taste with an unfunny remark. It's important that you care about having hurt someone's feelings. Otherwise, no matter what you say, they will know your heart's not in it. If you're thinking, "Lighten up, why don't you?" it will show.

A less-than-wholehearted apology might only worsen things:

"I didn't mean to. It was an accident."

"I don't know why you're upset—I didn't mean anything by it."

"It was just a slip of the tongue. What's the big deal?"

"You want blood or something? I *said* I'm sorry."

> One of the basic causes for all the trouble in the world today is that people talk too much and think too little.
> —MARGARET CHASE SMITH

If you are a compassionate person, you will feel bad about hurting someone's feelings and want to make amends.

Apologize with feeling, and your sincerity will show. Say something like:

"Could I delete that last scene?"

"Go ahead, tell me what you think of me!"

"How can I make amends?"

"I apologize for telling everyone your news before you could—I don't know what I was thinking."

"I didn't mean it the way it come out—I am so clumsy."

"I'm sorry—how incredibly thoughtless of me."

"I really goofed, and I'm so sorry."

> It's a fact that it is much more comfortable to be in the position of the person who has been offended than to be the unfortunate cause of it.
> —BARBARA WALTERS

"Is my face ever red!"

"It was my idea of a joke—a very bad idea."

"I was definitely out of line, and I apologize."

"I wouldn't blame you for being angry—I'd be angry too if I were you."

"I wouldn't hurt you for the world."

"Tactless and inappropriate hardly covers it—I am sorry."

"Tell me I didn't really say that. I'm so sorry."

> An apology is the superglue of life. It can repair just about anything.
> —LYNN JOHNSTON

"There is simply no good excuse for what I said."

"You were right, I was wrong, and I'm sorry."

When apologizing, apologize once and do it right, and then drop it. Don't keep bringing it up. In addition, avoid an overly dramatic, fulsome apology, for example:

"I am the worst klutz in the world."

"I am very, very, very sorry."

"I can't believe what a terrible, stupid, bad, irresponsible, hurtful, untrue, awful thing I said."

"I could kill myself for saying that!"

"I'm horribly ashamed. In fact, I think I'd better go home now."

"I wish I were dead after what I did."

"I wouldn't blame you a bit if you refused to ever speak with me again."

"These things always happen to me."

"This is the worst thing I've ever done."

"You'll probably never speak with me again."

If you are the person who has been hurt or insulted, forgive the other person on the spot, if you can. Recognize that people make mindless, stupid remarks they haven't thought through. With any luck, you've done the same thing yourself and understand how it can happen. Say something like:

The less said the better.
—JANE AUSTEN

"Don't give it another thought—but don't do it again!"

"I accept your apology."

"I've done the same thing."

"Let's just forget it."

"Thank you. I appreciate your apology."

You Blurt Out Someone's Secret

You certainly didn't mean to let the cat out of the bag: "But that's because she's pregnant. Oops!" "He didn't quit. He was fired. Um, but he said not to tell anyone."

Or, sometimes, perhaps you did mean to spill the beans. Perhaps you succumbed to the temptation to let people know that you knew a secret. Knowledge and information are power, but if people don't know you know things no one else does, what good is it? So you leak the news: "Now don't tell anyone, but she's divorcing him." "No one is supposed to know, but apparently he's being treated for kleptomania."

> *The etiquette business has its emergencies, heaven knows, but it is in the nature of etiquette emergencies that once one realizes what one has done, it is too late. One might as well get a good night's sleep and send flowers with an apology in the morning.*
>
> —JUDITH MARTIN

Telling another person's secret is a serious breach of ethics, loyalty, and common decency. Reparations are in order.

Apologize to the people in whom you confided the secret. Tell them you know how wrong it was to betray the other person and assure them that you will let the person know immediately what you've done. You need to make it right with the people who know you told a secret or they will never trust you themselves. If you acknowledge your wrong and regret it sincerely, they are likely to give you another chance.

As soon as possible, tell the person whose secret you betrayed what you have done. Apologize as sincerely as possible. Even if you told for venal motives (to appear "in the know," for example), you might tell the person it slipped out. Express profound regret.

You Tell a Truly Tasteless Joke

If you are oblivious enough to tell a tasteless joke, you might be oblivious to its effects on your listeners. On the other hand, their blank stares, uneasy laughter, and frowns might clue you in—or the fact that one or two immediately excuse themselves and leave your group.

Sometimes what is a hit in one group is tasteless in another. Know your listeners before telling a joke.

But you've goofed. What now?

Apologize briefly and sincerely. Do not hedge ("I didn't know you'd take it that way"; "Even though I still think it's funny, I'm sorry you didn't"). Then hope fervently that someone changes the subject. To apologize, you might say something like:

"I apologize."

"I don't know what I was thinking."

"If it's any consolation, I learned a lesson."

"I'm really sorry. I wasn't thinking."

"I'm sorry. I should have known better."

"I regret that."

"That was incredibly inappropriate, and I'm sorry."

He was, conversationally, a born elephant.
—Eleanor Dark

You Say Something Really Stupid

You have spoken disparagingly of fat cats in a group with two CEOs, of fat people in a group with several, and of your "fat chance" of getting a promotion within hearing of your boss. Besides being obsessed with fat, you have obviously not yet tamed that wild thing that is your tongue.

Or, you use the word "retard" and then discover that one of your listeners is the parent of a child with Down syndrome. You complain about a local city council member only to realize that her husband is standing next to you. You have such strong feelings about people who smoke and then have more illnesses, which costs all of us, that you take off on your rant without noticing the notorious smoker in the group.

The issue varies, but the result is the same: you would give anything to take back what you said. You can't, of course, and although you apologize, people will remember your gaffe. The best cure is prevention. Until you can trust your brain not to send every thought straight out your mouth, keep quiet or stick to the banal.

Silence is all the genius a fool has.
—Zora Neale Hurston

What do you do when it's too late for prevention? Apologize simply and earnestly. Your demeanor as much as your words should show that you realize your stupidity and regret it mightily:

"How incredibly stupid of me."

"I am an idiot, and I've just proved it."

"I am so sorry."

"Please forgive me. I don't know what I could have been thinking."

"Talk about thoughtless. Literally thoughtless. I apologize."

"That was not an appropriate thing to say. I should have realized it sooner."

"Will you forgive me for saying something so thoughtless?"

You Find the Conversation Extremely Unpleasant

The simplest response here is to flee. Mutter an excuse and leave the group or the person. Looking a little sick would help, and might not be that hard to do.

If you are trapped, however, say something like:

> *A general rule of etiquette is that one apologizes for the unfortunate occurrence, but the unthinkable is unmentionable.*
> —JUDITH MARTIN

"Could we change the subject? I'm feeling queasy."

"I did not need to hear that."

"I don't know about that, but there's one thing I do know: I'm hungry! Will you excuse me?"

"I don't need to know this, if you don't mind."

"I'm having a hard time listening to this—would you mind changing the subject?"

"I'm really uncomfortable with what you're saying."

"Pardon me, but that is waaaaay too much detail for me."

Someone Trashes Another Person's Reputation

You're chatting in a small group when one or two of the others start talking about someone known to you all. Their words are not charitable and they make you uncomfortable. What can you do?

Nobody likes to be thought a prig. On the other hand, if friends were speaking about you this way, you'd hope someone would put a stop to it. If the others aren't embarrassed by their boorish remarks, you needn't be embarrassed for standing up for your principles.

You can always excuse yourself and leave the group in such a way that your opinion is communicated. But it's probably more effective, and you'll feel better about it, if you feel able to say something like:

> *There are moments when silence becomes an unpardonable sin.*
> —MARY BOYLE O'REILLY

"And you believe all that?"

"Dear me, I feel as though I'm back in sixth grade."

"I could always ask him about this—maybe there's another side to the story."

"I don't have much patience with hearsay—it's unreliable."

"I'm surprised to hear you say that."

"I've always thought she was the nicest person—I really don't enjoy hearing this."

"Really. [Turning to another person] I've been wanting to ask you if you ever got those tickets to the jazz concert."

"Say, you won't mind if I mention that you said this, will you? He really should know what's being said."

"That's interesting because he always says such nice things about you."

Two People in Your Group Start Arguing

As entertaining as this can be for onlookers, it really doesn't belong at a business or social gathering.

You might be tempted to referee the argument, weighing in on the side of reason, fairness, and logic. But this is not likely to help. You are better off letting them know they are making the rest of you uncomfortable. You can also change the subject or separate them.

> *Their civil discussions weren't interesting, and their interesting discussions weren't civil.*
> —LISA ALTHER

You might address one of the combatants with something like:

"Excuse me, can you show me where the restroom is?"

"Gene, would you please get me a napkin? I've spilled my coffee."

"I promised to find someone to serve refreshments with me—would you mind helping out?"

"Say, I hate to interrupt, but I've been wanting to ask if I can borrow your belt sander for a few days."

Or you could address them both:

"All right then, one two three, a change of subject has been decreed!"

"Can we please change the subject? This isn't fun anymore."

"Can we table this issue for now? This isn't the right place for it."

"Could you continue with that some other time? I need to ask you a few questions about the Get Out the Vote campaign."

> "Excuse me for interrupting, but I think we ought to check out the buffet before the food disappears."
>
> "Hey, you guys, you're making the rest of us uncomfortable."
>
> "My dad always told me not to talk politics. You two are the perfect example why."
>
> "Pardon me for interrupting, but I wondered if you noticed that the rest of us aren't enjoying ourselves as much as you are."
>
> "Say, why don't you two step outside and settle this?"

You Get Into an Argument

All right, it wasn't your fault, and you didn't start it, and you normally wouldn't be speaking this loudly or be this upset, but somebody had to put that So-and-So in their place.

However it began, whatever it is about, a public argument will not enhance your reputation. As soon as you are reasonable enough to realize that you're in the midst of a dust-up, get yourself out of it. Forget about winning or losing the argument, forget about who's right, forget everything except that you will always look like a loser for arguing in front of others.

On your way out of the argument, do what you can to help the other person save face. Everyone will feel better if you do. Say something like:

> *Even when you think people are wrong, it is easy to tell when they are right. When they are right about something you are trying very hard to hide from others and yourself, you know they are right because you want to kill them.*
>
> —CANDICE BERGEN

> "I need to get something to eat immediately. Maybe we can pick up where we left off some other time."
>
> "I think we agree on more than we appear to. Let's call it a tie."
>
> "Let's continue this later—after I check out the refreshment table."
>
> "We covered a lot of ground. May I get you a fresh drink?"
>
> "We've clarified a few things, which is good, and now I need a cup of coffee."
>
> "You've made some good points. I'll think about them."

There are individuals who enjoy arguing simply for the fun of it. They can take either side of an issue because the issue doesn't matter as much as arguing does. If this is you, cease and desist, except in the rare instance when you find someone who enjoys debating as much as you do. Ordinarily, bystanders find these exchanges uncomfortable and the person you're arguing with gets riled up because they don't realize it's an entertainment for you. Keep it for family and friends.

Someone Asks You for Professional Advice

You know enough not to expect to get professional advice for nothing—and after hours, at that. But not everyone does.

You work for an art museum, and at a party someone approaches you and says they have a painting out in the car that might be valuable. Could you take a look? You're a professor of geology, and someone pulls a handful of stones and a pen and notebook from their pocket and asks if you would please identify them. Because you are fluent in Greek, a friend shows you a letter written by a Greek business client and asks you to translate it on the spot.

You need not and should not respond to such requests, even when they come from people you like. Imagine what they're going to pull out at the next party for some other expert trying to relax! They must be taught—gently—that this is unacceptable. Say something like:

> "I'd love to help but you'll have to set up an appointment with my assistant. Here's my card."
>
> "I'm off duty now. Call me tomorrow about finding a time when I'm wearing my professional hat."
>
> "I need to do that at the office. Sorry."
>
> "I try to keep work for work hours."
>
> "Oh, I couldn't possibly do that without my dictionary/microscope/reference works."
>
> "That's what I do all day long. I know you'll understand if I say I'm finished for the day. Try me at the office sometime."
>
> "You know, I came here tonight to relax, and that would not relax me!"

Someone Asks You an Inappropriate Question

How much money do you make? Why did you get divorced? Are you a Democrat or a Republican? Have you accepted Jesus as your Savior? Do you carry life insurance? How did you get that scar? I never see your wife anymore—what's going on?

Questions like these need never be answered, and certainly shouldn't be asked. But society has become so open that people appear on national television to tell what would once have been kept strictly to oneself or at least in the family. It's not surprising that some people assume everyone is willing to let it all hang out.

To avoid answering a question without appearing guilty, secretive, or disagreeable:

- Return the ball to the other person's court: "Do you need to know this?" "Why do you want to know?" "Why do you ask?" If they shrug it off with, "Just curious," you can respond with a flat, "Really," and change the subject.
- Without answering the question, change the subject: "Speaking of salaries, did you see what we're paying the mayor?" "My wife? That reminds me, I finally met the wife of our CEO."
- You can say, "That's not something I talk about. I'd rather hear about the bears in the neighborhood."
- You can refuse to answer but in a way that does not imply, "You idiot, why are you asking me this?": "I find that a difficult question to answer." "Oh, I never tell that." "I'd rather not get into that." "My mother made me promise never to tell." "I'd rather hear how you got into your line of work."
- Act as if you didn't hear the question and toss something completely random or inane into the conversation: "I don't suppose you know a good way of getting rid of potato bugs." "Say! I won ten dollars in the football pool."

Silence is a good response, if you are the kind of person who can do this. Look around the room, smiling slightly. The other person will wait to see if you are going to respond. Before they repeat the question, you can introduce another topic.

Much of good manners is about knowing when to pretend that what's happening isn't happening.
—Mrs. Falk Feeley

Someone's Conversation Carries Sexual Innuendo

A few people remain confused about the difference between friendly, appreciative remarks and sexual innuendo. In the workplace, unwelcome, unsolicited, nonreciprocated sexual advances, requests for sexual favors, sexually motivated physical contact, or communication of a sexual nature, usually by someone who has power over another person, are all called sexual harassment. This includes comments, jokes, looks, and physical contact. It emphasizes a person's sex role over their function as a worker. And it is against the law.

If you are on the receiving end of such behavior, say something like:

"Do you know that your behavior toward me constitutes sexual harassment?"

"I consider your behavior sexual harassment. Please speak to me in a professional and respectful manner."

"No. You will not use language like that to speak with me."

"Please do not speak to me like that. If it happens again, I will have to report it to Ms. Ossifer."

"There are sites on the Internet that will explain to you that your behavior toward me is sexual harassment. You can also find out there how you can be fired and prosecuted for it. Do yourself a favor and get educated on the subject."

For speech and actions that are not stopped by a verbal request, see your company's policy on sexual harassment and pursue the options available.

Outside the workplace, leave immediately if you feel threatened or harassed by someone's conversation. They will get the point.

You Are Trapped by a Tireless Talker

You have been taken prisoner by The Unrelenting One. With smiles and flashing hands and gimlet eyes, this adroit marathoner of the spoken word seamlessly weaves one tale into the next and into the next. Should your eyes wander for a second, the person brings you back by using your name: "And then, Julie—you'll like this next part—" If you try to interrupt, they say, "Yes, yes, but first listen to this."

Her tongue is hung in de middle and works both ways.
—Zora Neale Hurston

You know that no one will come to your rescue because they don't want to be in your shoes. You will have to save yourself.

Conjuring up an emergency of some sort will free you while helping the other person save face. You will probably have to interrupt to say something like:

"Good grief! I missed my medication an hour ago. Excuse me, I must take it immediately."

"I forgot to leave a number where the sitter can reach us. Excuse me while I give her a call."

> *He talks for the pleasure of his own voice, the way dogs bark and birds sing.*
> —PAULETTE BATES ALDEN

"I've taken far too much of your time, and now I'm late. Good-bye!"

"My cell is vibrating—the only person who'd call me here is my mother—I'd better take this."

"Oh no! My eBay auction ends in a few minutes. Will you excuse me?"

"We'll finish this some other time. For now I've got to run."

(See Chapter 1, "Ending a Conversation," for additional suggestions.)

CHAPTER 8

How to Be an Unpopular Conversationalist

> *The real art of conversation is not only to say the right thing in the right place, but, far more difficult still, to leave unsaid the wrong thing at the tempting moment.*
>
> —Dorothy Nevill

Becoming a charming conversationalist doesn't always mean learning new tricks, adopting carefully studied behaviors, or adding to your repertoire of conversational gambits. Successful conversing can also be a case of "less is more." Simply cutting out some of your less appealing habits can make you a candidate for "most popular" at any gathering.

Are You Boring?

Dorothy Carnegie says, "Nobody ever bores another on purpose." But she adds, "You and I, horrible thought, may be a bore without knowing it."

How do you know if you're boring? Your listeners' smiles are frozen in place, their eyes wander, they attempt to interrupt you, they rock restlessly from side to side, and they glance surreptitiously at their watches. They look desperate.

> *Don't go on endlessly about your operation, and describe every twinge you had from the time you entered the hospital until you went back to work. Telling about how much you suffered won't make you a hero. It will only make you a bore.*
>
> —Lee Giblin

Bores are almost always motormouths. They go on and on and on. And on. They segue from one sentence to the next, from one paragraph to the next without, as far as anyone can tell, taking a breath. Onlookers wait, equally breathlessly, for the merest opening in the spate of words, but it never comes.

Single-mindedness can also be boring, unless you are with people who share your passion. Some people have a positive genius for bringing any conversation directly back to their own fixation: "Funny you should mention pineapples because in my collection of paperweights...."

Belaboring a favored topic does not constitute conversation. You are merely talking at someone, not with him.
—BERNARDO J. CARDUCCI

"Did you say nuclear waste? Well, although I don't have any paperweights containing nuclear waste, I do have one with some ashes from Mount Helen." "Your new car sounds wonderful. Did I tell you I have a whole series of paperweights with tiny convertibles in them?"

Check yourself now and then to see if you tend to circle around the same topic every time you speak.

Half the world is composed of people who have something to say and can't, and the other half who have nothing to say and keep on saying it.
—ROBERT FROST

Overexplaining is often boring for listeners. Watch to see if you're saying the same thing, only in different words and, then again, in still other words. Bores often talk a topic to death with repetition and overexplaining. Watch your listeners' faces for comprehension. If they say, "I see," they probably do, so advance to the next point.

Do You Monopolize the Conversation?

One of the most popular ways of boring people is to monopolize the conversation. Celestine Sibley describes a woman who "handles a conversation like the only runner in a potato race. She offers you the potato and before you can take it she's turned and rushed off with it again herself."

Craddock thinks a conversation consists of him talking and everybody else nodding.
—CAROLINE LLEWELLYN

How do you know you're monopolizing the conversation? Your own wristwatch will tell you. If you have been holding the floor for longer than two or three minutes, it's time for someone else to talk.

In addition, people who monopolize the conversation never ask questions of the others. They answer their own questions themselves, ignore newcomers to the group, and keep talking no matter what is going on.

Have you ever seen a person talk on and on, and you can tell by the rather frantic look in their eyes that they know they are monopolizing the conversation, but don't quite know how to get off the horse?

If you find yourself talking nonstop, abruptly ask something like:

> *Whether in private conversation or in a group—if you are doing all the talking, you are boring somebody!*
> —HELEN GURLEY BROWN

"Did you ever travel there?"

"Do you collect anything yourself?"

"Has this ever happened to you?"

"What do you think about this?"

"What's your opinion?"

"What would you have done?"

No one will notice that you cut yourself off in the middle of your spiel because they'll be busy thinking about the question. And then, no matter how much you want to add something or—worse yet—finish what you were saying, resist the temptation to take the conversation back. Remember that, in the metaphor of sports, a conversation is neither a potato race nor a golf game; it is a tennis match, so make sure the ball goes back and forth—it shouldn't stay on your side all the time.

There are times when a person monopolizes the conversation, and every listener is delighted with the situation. If you are honest with yourself when you read your audience's faces, you will know if you are a delight or a bore.

> *It is not the correct thing to invite many people who like to monopolize conversation; one of this kind will be found amply sufficient.*
> —FLORENCE HOWE HALL

A subsection of those who monopolize a conversation are those who are dogmatic and didactic. They have opinions and you are going to hear them. What's more, you are going to be told you should, indeed must, adopt them for your own. Preachy, a bit hectoring, and full of their own righteousness, these people take the floor and consider it only good and proper to be listened to with deference. You could not be one of these. But do nip any little tendencies toward didacticism in the bud.

One way some people inadvertently monopolize a conversation is in not knowing how to tell a story in a straightforward manner. They obsess about whether it all happened on a Tuesday or a Wednesday or perhaps even on Thursday. Meanwhile their listeners have already decided they wish it hadn't happened at all. The storyteller goes on to try to determine whether it was the barber or the dog who barked, and the exact sequence of the stuck player piano and the pomegranate exploding in the microwave.

A convenient guideline is that no story, no matter how involved or funny or interesting, should take more than two or three minutes to tell.

Do You Interrupt?

If you've ever been interrupted when you're trying to get an idea across, you know how frustrating it is.

Interrupters specialize in irrelevant questions ("Where did you buy that lawn mower?"), pointless remarks ("When you're finished, I want to tell you about the time something similar happened to me"), completing sentences for others ("I picked up a..." "Hammer? Spatula? Fly swatter?" "...a staple gun..."), helping to tell your story ("So then you probably called 911, right?"), or to dispute trivial details ("Oh, no, it must've been a .244 because they didn't make the .245 until 1997, although...").

> *I know of no quicker way to insult a person or to hurt his feelings than to interrupt him when he's trying to tell you something.*
> —JAMES K. VAN FLEET

Some people interrupt because of nervous temperaments—they can't wait for speakers to finish their sentences, or their brain flashes news of a connection to something they know, and having all the impulse control of a mousetrap, anything that passes through their brain immediately comes out their mouth. They might have the best intentions and be the innocents of the conversational world. They are still very, very irritating.

If you're guilty of this kind of interrupting, it's difficult to interrupt yourself, as it were. The solution is to strictly refrain from opening your mouth when anyone is speaking. It's easier to stop yourself before you begin than it is to catch yourself after you've already interrupted. Clutch a coin in one hand or in your pocket to remind you to keep quiet.

Other interrupters want to control the conversation. They need to continually put their stamp, their mark, on all that is said. Interrupting puts the speaker at a disadvantage, so the interrupter appears more powerful.

> *Only if we can restrain ourselves is conversation possible. Good talk rises upon much self-discipline.*
> —JOHN ERSKINE

If you are this type of interrupter, you might want to evaluate the success of your tactic. Are you better liked? Are you indeed more powerful? Is interrupting working for you? Most truly powerful individuals are so confident of their power that they have no need to display it in trivial ways.

A few interruptions are allowed everyone, especially those interruptions that result from a genuine excitement about what's being said. You can tell the "good" interruptions from the "bad" interruptions because the former push speakers forward and allow them to quickly resume what they were saying. The latter stalls out the conversation and the speaker finds it awkward regaining momentum.

If you are conscientious about not interrupting others, you might find yourself particularly irritated and angry at those who interrupt you, especially when you are fairly certain you are not monopolizing the conversation or boring anyone. How do you continue in the face of interruptions?

Try saying something like:

"As I was saying…"

"Going back to what I was saying…"

"I didn't finish what I was saying."

"I didn't get to elaborate about my reasons."

"If I may continue…?"

"I'm not finished."

"I still want to explain why I feel that way."

"I want to hear what you're saying, but first I…"

"Let me finish my thought and then you can have the floor."

"Let me get to the main point."

"May I finish this thought?"

"Pardon me, I'm not finished."

"To get back to my point…"

"Yes, but then…"

When you're a bystander and see someone get interrupted, it would be kind of you to redirect the conversation: "You were saying...?" or "What happened then?" or "You were starting to tell us...?"

Is Your Speech Marked by Verbal Tics?

Most of us have a few repetitive speech habits that we are scarcely aware of. Unfortunately, other people notice them. Ask someone who loves you if they've observed you relying on the same expressions...and get rid of them, or use them only rarely.

One of the most annoying phrases, "To make a long story short..." is used by people who, oddly enough, have no concept of a short story; this expression serves merely as an apology for the long story that is to follow. If you find yourself using "To make a long story short..." check to see if yours are some of the longest stories around. And trim them.

The following phrases are fine when used once in a conversation. Used over and over, they become both meaningless and irritating to your listener:

"Actually"

"Am I not right?"

"Are you clear to this point?"

"Are you with me?"

"As you know"

"Basically"

"Blah, blah, blah"

"Correct?"

"Etcetera, etcetera, etcetera"

"Hmm"

"If you know what I mean"

"I go"

"I mean"

"In any event"

"Is that clear?"

"Like"

"Naturally"

"Of course"

"Okay?"

"Really"

"Right?"

"See what I'm saying?"

"So to speak"

"Think about it!"

"To make a long story short"

"Uh"

"Ultimately"

"Um"

"Well"

"Yadda, yadda, yadda"

"You follow me?"

"You got that?"

"You know"

"You know what I mean?"

"You understand?"

What should you use instead? Nothing. These phrases, especially when repeated, add absolutely zilch to your conversation.

Another verbal tic varies with the individual. For some it's the word *cute*. Or the word *nice*. For others it's *gross* or *great* or *awesome*. Once some people find a word like *egregious*, they will use it every few minutes. It gets old. Have a friend or relative check you for tics.

Do You Make Sweeping Generalizations?

No one likes a generalization. That is, almost no one. As soon as you use words like *always* or *never*, people begin to bristle and to tell you that actually once they did win the office pool or take a vacation or wear a tie to work.

Another kind of generalization is attributing to a whole set of people the attributes of a few of them. For example, "Women are terrible drivers" or "Smokers are so insensitive" or "Single men live like bears with furniture." Some women. Some smokers. Some single men. Even people who aren't women, smokers, or single men will bristle at the blanket condemnations.

Watch your use of:

"All"
"Always"
"Constantly"
"Continually"
"Everyone"
"Every single time"
"Everything"
"Every time"
"In no case"
"Invariably"
"Never"
"None"
"Not in a million years"
"Repeatedly"
"Totally"
"Under no circumstances"
"Without exception"

Use instead:

"A few"
"A great many"
"Frequently"
"Generally"
"Infrequently"
"Many"
"Most often"
"Occasionally"
"Often"
"Once in a while"
"Ordinarily"

"Some"

"Sometimes"

"Usually"

Do You Give or Ask for Advice?

You might not realize that you appear preachy, patronizing, and superior, but if you use words like "ought" and "should," you are probably annoying your listener.

If asked for advice—and, in most cases, it is better to wait until you are positively begged for advice—you can use less aggressive words.

Some people really want advice, but some people only want you to tell them, "You're doing everything right!" or "Well, what a dreadful situation. I'm so sorry."

> *It's awfully important to know what is and what is not your business.*
> —GERTRUDE STEIN

Watch your use of:

"Better not"

"Had better"

"Have to"

"If I were you, I'd"

"Must"

"Ought to"

"Should"

"Shouldn't"

"You'd be crazy to"

Use instead:

"Could look into"

"Have you thought about"

"I might mention that"

"I might suggest"

"In my opinion"

"It seems to me"

"I wonder if"

"One idea to consider"

"This is just my opinion, but"

"What if you"

"What you could try"

"You might want to"

"You've probably thought of this, but"

Asking a friend's advice is entirely acceptable. However, at a social or business event, it is totally unacceptable to ask a carpenter, lawyer, accountant, nurse, horse trainer, or anyone with a specialty, for professional advice.

Do You Protest Too Much?

Have you ever conversed with someone whose every other word was "frankly" or "honestly"? Some people seem to need to preface every remark with an assurance of their candor. This is not only irritating and unnecessary (conversations are not contracts), but it often makes you wonder why they need to bring it up all the time.

Watch your use of:

"Candidly"

"Frankly"

"Honestly"

"I like plain dealing"

"In all honesty"

"In all seriousness"

"I sincerely mean that"

"I truly believe"

"Let's be honest"

"Let's be honest about it"

"May I be frank?"

"To be perfectly honest with you"

"To tell the truth"

"Truthfully"

> *Smart people duck when they hear the dread announcement "I'm going to be perfectly honest with you."*
> —JUDITH MARTIN

Use instead:

Nothing. Omit all protestations of your honesty.

Do You Tell Secrets?

You know better, of course. But every once in a while, you can't help it. You give in to the desire to be the one who knows what no one else does.

It's no good swearing to secrecy the recipient of the secret that wasn't-yours-to-tell. This is not in the implied covenant you have with the person who has the secret. You know this, but you hope to have your cake and it eat too: you get credit for sharing the secret, while the other person swears not to tell. Consider that that promise is worth just about what yours was.

It hardly needs to be said, but spilling secrets will make you very unpopular indeed, and it's no good hoping that no one will know. They know.

In the business world, it is essential to treat with absolute discretion any information you are entrusted with. Here it is not a case of being popular but a case of being employed. You could end up un-.

> *She had seen enough of the world to know that in few people is discretion stronger than the desire to tell a good story.*
> —LADY MURASAKI

> *A person who tells a secret, swearing the recipient to secrecy in turn, is asking of the other person a discretion which he is abrogating himself.*
> —DOROTHY L. SAYERS AND JILL PATON WALSH

Is Your Conversation Always Top-Secret?

Some people seem to need to endow every conversation with an atmosphere of secrecy. They convey that you and only you are privy to this information—even when it's trivial and unimportant. They lower their voice to a whisper and lean toward you. Their conversations are larded with "just between you and me and the lamp post." If you are one of these people, get over it. This mannerism is irritating, and few people believe that what you are saying is privileged information.

Watch your use of:

"Between ourselves"

"Between you and me"

"Between you and me and the lamp post"

"Confidentially"

"Entre nous"

"For your ears only"

"In strict confidence"

"Just between us"

"Keep it under your hat"

"Off the record"

"Strictly between us"

Instead use:

Nothing. Omit all references to confidentiality. Watch how other people speak in matter-of-fact tones, and go and do likewise.

Do You Gossip?

Depending on how you define it, gossip is not a bad thing. J.E. Buckrose said, "The right sort of gossip is a charming and stimulating thing. The *Odyssey* itself is simply glorious gossip, and the same may be said of nearly every tale of mingled fact and legend which has been handed down to us through the ages."

At the very least, gossip is "just the small change of conversation" (Rae Foley). All that said, passing on rumors or talking about the personal, intimate, or sensationalistic actions of other people is better avoided.

It might make you look good at the moment, as other people seem to like to hear these things. But later you will assume a rather sinister cast in other people's memories—another case of the messenger's unpopularity.

Liz Smith, popular gossip columnist for many years, says "Bad gossip drives out good gossip." Passing on news of others' achievements—and even the sometimes interesting stories of how they managed it—is very nice "gossip" indeed. News of those whose health has improved,

---

Malicious gossip...takes the place of creation in noncreative lives.
—NANCY HALE

who have bought a new business or new house, or who've added to their family is, strictly speaking, gossip, but eminently acceptable.

Being able to distinguish between harmless talk about others ("Cecil and Ann are in Thailand for a month") and unpleasant talk about others ("I guess he's taking her for every cent she's got") is a social skill that you should not have to learn the hard way.

The quick test of whether your piece of news is acceptable in a group is to ask yourself what the objects of the news would think if they could overhear you. Would they be glad their friends were thinking about them, or would smoke be coming out of their ears?

You can tell when you're gossiping negatively when you say things like:

"Did you hear about Keisha?"

"Do you know why Felix hasn't been at work lately?"

"I don't suppose you heard the latest about Mert."

"Wait until I tell you what Stephanie did."

"You won't believe what I heard about Dennis."

Positive gossiping sounds more like this:

"Good news! Jennie got engaged and he is a prince of a fellow."

"I guess the Chesters are going to buy a ranch in Montana—I wonder how they'll adjust from the big city to such a remote area."

"I heard that Hank is finally home and feeling strong enough to have visitors."

"Say, the new tech apparently plays a tidy game of tennis—we can use another good player."

Along with gossiping, a lack of discretion can be a big minus in a conversationalist. Don't, for example, discuss situations that belong in the office at a social gathering, mention a party the others weren't invited to, or tell how much another person paid for something. Ask yourself if the person standing across from you would be likely to say such a thing. If not, don't.

Do You Brag and One-Up Others?

The whole point of conversation is to find out a little about the other person, so people truly want to know something about you. From there to painting yourself as a Renaissance woman, superman, folk hero, or award-winning all-around human being is something else.

There's a fine line between telling about yourself and describing yourself in superlatives. It's important that you reveal who you are in small ways, and it's even interesting for other people to hear about your successes—if you know how to both entertain and inspire them in the process.

People want to hear your opinions and ideas, but in recounting them try not to place yourself at the center of the universe. A Reader's Digest publication, *Write Better, Speak Better*, advises, "Don't talk in such a way that your topics can be described as 'the Pyrenees and me,' 'inflation and me,' 'the Taj Mahal and me,' 'the Supreme Court and me,' 'the decimal point and me,' etc."

> *Modest egotism is the salt of conversation. You do not want too much of it; but if it is altogether omitted, everything tastes flat.*
> —HENRY VAN DYKE

▶ Stay with the facts and let others draw the conclusions. Instead of saying, "I'm one of their top people. In fact, I was Sales Rep of the Year in 2004," say, "I'm in software sales, and I really enjoy my work." Your attitude will give the idea that you are successful at what you do. Later, after you know the person better, you can let them know about your great 2004 year.

▶ Instead of mentioning your accomplishments ("I was a million-dollar seller last year"), talk about what fascinates you about your work ("I've been keeping records to see how many houses, on average, a person looks at before coming to the point of buying"). Again, later, when the other person presses you for more information—as they're likely to do—you can confess how well you did last year.

> *Egotism—usually just a case of mistaken nonentity.*
> —BARBARA STANWYCK

▶ Instead of using "I," ally yourself with others when it's appropriate: "Several of us decided the neighborhood children should have a park." In the other person's mind, you will receive most of the credit for this, but it sounds so much less egocentric.

▶ Some people identify closely with the speaker. Unfortunately, however, they can't help jumping in after every other sentence with a "me, too": "Oh, me too! We bought one of the first ones and..." "Yeah, I know what you mean—I had a guy like that who worked for me and let me tell you..." "That very thing happened to me, except that..." "I thought it was great too—in fact, I went out and bought the whole series and...."

It's helpful to a conversation to indicate you're "with" the other person. However, you shouldn't grab the conversation and turn it to your own purposes. Let the other person tell their story their own way.

▶ In the same way, allow the other person to relate an experience without trying to trump it with yours: "That's nothing! You should hear what happened to me when I was in Cairo!" Your experience might be fifty times more amazing than theirs, but save it for another time. No matter how incredible it was, the other person is not going to like you better for stealing their bit of thunder.

Do You Complain?

Unless you can complain in an entertaining manner, leave your complaints at home. One or two complaints, especially those shared by the people with whom you're talking, are usually fine: "What are we going to do about the photocopying machine? Has it ever worked properly?"

It is the habitual complainer who is shunned like a trans-fatty acid. Their litany of complaints is known to all their acquaintances: people who enter the freeway at forty miles an hour, the humidity, the poor design of car engines, the leaky sink in the restroom, long lines at the post office, being put on hold after going through fifteen automated menus. Here's the thing: this is not very interesting. Everyone runs into the same annoyances, but most people have better things to talk about.

> *I personally think we developed language because of our deep inner need to complain.*
> —JANE WAGNER

You might not even know you are a complainer. But if you are not the most popular card in the deck, you might ask yourself why. Check your last conversation to see how much of it was complaining.

Do You Put Down Other People and Their Ideas?

You might feel that people should be able to take constructive criticism. If not, what are they doing in this business? And so you lay about you with your opinions on other people's ideas and work. You might even have some excellent critiques to offer. Without phrasing them tactfully, however, few people will come to you for feedback.

Or you actually think you're being helpful and have no idea how negative you are most of the time. Sometimes intelligent people see more sides to a situation than others do. However, in a conversation, refrain from bringing up the down side of every discussion.

Avoid critical, bubble-bursting put-downs like:

"Are you out of your mind? The board will never go for that."

"As someone who's been here a lot longer than you have, I can tell you that's not going to fly."

"As you'll soon discover, it's not that easy."

"But that's ridiculous!"

"Didn't you know that? Huh! I thought everyone knew that."

"I can top that!"

"I'll tell you what's scary, I mean, *really* scary."

"I'm glad you're happy with it, but you paid about $50 more than you had to."

"I sold my first book when I was eight years younger than you are."

"I suppose you had no way of knowing, but that story is an urban myth."

"It may interest you to know that we already tried that—it's a dead end."

"I wouldn't try that, if I were you."

"That reminds me of what happened to me."

"That will never work. Believe me, I've been over it and I know it'll never work."

"Wait until you hear *our* sales figures!"

"We stayed there before it was overrun by tourists—you should have seen it then."

"When I was your age, I already had three children and a mortgage."

"You actually think that's a good deal?"

"You ate where? Oh, that's a terrible place. You should've gone across the street to the little bistro."

Do You Put Yourself Down?

You might think it is charmingly modest to put yourself down, but it makes others uncomfortable. Or you might feel the need to excuse yourself more than the situation calls for. This also makes listeners uneasy.

Many of us preface most of our speech with self-effacing caveats. It is difficult to rid your speech of a habit that probably goes back to childhood, but make an effort. Those little "humble" introductions lengthen your sentences unnecessarily and make you sound as though you think you're pretty dumb. Let other people decide. This is a case of people taking you at your evaluation of yourself. If you apologize enough, people will begin to think you have a lot to apologize for.

> *Don't pass judgment upon yourself. People are not especially interested in what you think of your own character or personality.*
>
> —Lillian Eichler

Avoid prefatory phrases like:

"Excuse me for asking the obvious, but..."

"I know this is probably a stupid question, but..."

"I'm probably wrong about this, but..."

"I'm sorry to seem so dense, but..."

"I'm sure everyone else knows the answer to this question, but..."

"I probably shouldn't bring this up, but..."

"I probably shouldn't say anything, but..."

"Not that I know anything about this, but..."

"This question is probably a waste of time, but..."

"This will sound dumb, but..."

"You probably already told us this, but..."

Instead, delete your opening phrase and go directly to your question or statement:

"How was that done?"

"I didn't get that idea from what she said."

"I thought that had been outlawed."

"I understood it showed up in red rather than in purple."

"What did you mean by...?"

"Who was responsible?"

"Why did it work the second time?"

"Will you explain how...?"

Do You Misuse Words?

Correct grammar and word pronunciation are subjects for other books. However, there are a handful of words that are commonly misused or overused in everyday conversations.

- *Between you and me* is always correct. *Between you and I* is never correct. Never. People will also say things like, "They gave a party for Jill and I" or "They gave a present to Jill and I." Ouch! Whenever you have a preposition (*between, for, to*), it takes the objective pronoun. But never mind the grammar lesson. Just remember that you would never say, "They gave a party for I" or "They gave a present to I." If this is an error of yours, practice saying, "Between you and me" until it sounds right to you.

- *Like* is misused in ways we are all familiar with: "I'm, like, wow, is that ever great" and "I was like, why doesn't he move!" You know better than to use it that way except when you are with friends and family. But what is too often heard at social or business events is: "I felt like I should help her." *Like* is only used to compare something to a noun. So, if you like, you may say:

"I felt like a movie star."

"I felt like a winner."

"I felt like a worm."

You always feel like some*thing*. When another clause is involved, use *as if* or *as though*:

Whatever its function,
Like's not a conjunction.
—Margaret Fishback

"I felt as if I should help her."

"I felt as though the sky was falling."

"I felt as if the project was already doomed."

"I felt as though we were never going to make it."

- *Literally* is often misused to emphasize an action. Unless you are confident about the use of this word, strike it from your vocabulary. It's a lot easier to do that than to try to remember when to use it.

The word *literally* means *in actual fact* or *in reality* or *really and truly*. When someone says, "He literally bit my head off!" you know that the person didn't pay attention in English class. Of course, if you are a bat, and "he" was Ozzie Osbourne, you could correctly say (if you could still speak), "He literally bit my head off!"

People say things like "My head literally exploded." I don't think so. "The roof was literally shaking from his snores." Probably not.

- *Basically* is another word that you'd be best off striking from your vocabulary. It basically doesn't add anything to a sentence. Think of any sentence you like with *basically* in it, take it out, and see if the sentence doesn't sound the same.

- *Badly* is badly misused, primarily in this way: "I felt badly for him." No, you felt *bad* for him. "I felt badly about their burglary." No, you felt *bad* about their burglary. *Badly* is an adverb, so if you feel badly, it means that your fingertips are toughened or insensitive and you can't feel very well with them.

- *Utilize* is the most unnecessary word on the planet. No matter where you want to use *utilize*, use *use* instead. Please. It has crept in because some people think it sounds more high-tech or a little more "professional." No, it sounds silly. Use *use*.

- *Hopefully* has been much talked about. If you sin in this respect, it isn't the worst thing you can do. But wouldn't it be nice if more people used it correctly? *Hopefully* means *in a manner full of hope*. So, if you accidentally fall into quicksand, you will look hopefully about you for a long stick or a rescuer. *Hopefully* does not mean *I hope*. The common error is to say "Hopefully traffic isn't too stopped up tonight" or "Hopefully they'll sign the contract today" or "Hopefully the roof wasn't affected." What is meant in all these cases is: "I hope traffic isn't too stopped up tonight," "I hope they'll sign the contract today," and "I hope the roof wasn't affected."

- *Whomever* is scarcely ever used correctly. The odds are that if you always use *whoever*, you will almost always be correct. Once in a while, you will be wrong, but don't worry about it—it won't sound nearly as awful as a misused *whomever*. If you use *whomever*, however, you are almost always going to be wrong. Where people err is when *whoever* is the subject of a clause. For example, "I'd like to speak with whoever is in charge." Most people would say *whomever*, thinking that the issue is "with whom." No, the issue is a clause that says, "who is in charge."

This is not a comprehensive list of misused words, but thinking about them might make you more aware of words in general. A well-spoken conversationalist is comfortable and self-confident.

In addition, avoid jargon, computerese, pompous language, and unnecessarily big words.

If this is your normal manner of speech, enjoy it. If, however, you are making an effort to sound clever or learned and you have to work at including big words in your talk, don't.

Using big words can confuse listeners and make you appear pretentious or even foolish if you misuse them. Furrowed brows, glassy eyes, or uncertain grins could signal that you need to use more down-to-earth terms.

> *A great many people think that polysyllables are a sign of intelligence.*
> —BARBARA WALTERS

In a related shortcoming, some people who have learned a foreign language and are terribly proud of it like to toss a few *je ne sais quoi* into a conversation. If this is you, find a French friend and leave others alone.

Do You End Statements on a Questioning Note?

Letting your voice rise at the end of a statement so that it sounds like a question tells people that you are unsure of yourself. It also becomes annoying over time. Consider the difference between these pairs:

"I don't know."
"I don't know?"

"Here they come."
"Here they come?"

"I thought we could go to the park."
"I thought we could go to the park?"

"My favorite flavor is Rocky Road."
"My favorite flavor is Rocky Road?"

Do You Fail to Finish Your Sentences?

Trailing off—failing to finish your thoughts in complete sentences—makes listeners think you lack conviction or that you're not knowledgeable about your subject. Avoid sounding like this:

"I don't know, I thought maybe we could just..."

"If they don't accept this contract, we might, well, we might..."

"I mostly like their music. It's just that sometimes..."

"I suppose we could, although..."

"Sure, I used to, I mean..."

"What I was going to say was, well, you know..."

Would Jonathan Swift Have Approved of You?

Evaluating standards of good conversation is not a contemporary issue. In 1738, Jonathan Swift wrote an essay about polite conversation that is still relevant:

> Nothing is more generally exploded than the Folly of Talking too much, yet I rarely remember to have seen five People together, where some one among them hath not been predominant in that Kind, to the great Constraint and Disgust of all the rest. But among such as deal in Multitudes of Words, none are comparable to the sober deliberate Talker, who proceedeth with much Thought and Caution, maketh his Preface, brancheth out into several Digressions, findeth a Hint that putteth him in Mind of another Story, which he promiseth to tell you when this is done; cometh back regularly to his Subject, cannot readily call to Mind some Person's Name, holdeth his Head, complaineth of his Memory; the whole Company all this while in Suspence; at length says, it is no Matter, and so goes on. And, to crown the Business, it perhaps proveth at last a Story the Company hath heard fifty Times before; or, at best, some insipid Adventure of the Relater. Another general Fault in Conversation is, That of those who affect to talk of themselves: Some, without any Ceremony, will run over the History of their Lives; will relate the Annals of their Diseases, with the several Symptoms and Circumstances of them; will enumerate the Hardships and Injustice they have suffered in Court, in Parliament, in Love, or in Law.

Part Two

The Specifics

CHAPTER 9

Talking With Anyone in the Workplace

> *The brain is a wonderful organ; it starts working the moment you get up in the morning, and does not stop until you get into the office.*
> —ROBERT FROST

Introduction

Conversations at work can either support morale, efficiency, and teamwork—or undermine all three. It's too often ignored as a positive or negative factor in the business environment.

Workplace talk is necessarily short and superficial for the simple reason that no one was hired to stand around and chat.

On the other hand, although what Manutius says is, in many ways, correct, conversation at work has other important functions. Most workplace talk is structured (someone calls you, you call them, or you meet with another person or group, always to discuss something specific), but good things can happen in those odd moments when you stop to chat with someone.

> *Talk of nothing but business, and dispatch that business quickly.*
> —ALDUS MANUTIUS

> *We can assume that about half of the talking most of us do is in the course of our jobs. Time is money—don't waste time of business people you're talking to.*
> —LARRY KING

As it turns out, conversation is often not a waste of anyone's time when you consider its benefits as an alternative to the memo, letter, scheduled meeting, or phone call. You can get a lot of points across, with fewer negative feelings, by couching your message in a friendly conversation.

Conversation among workers and between management and workers can spark ideas, clarify murky situations, and build companywide loyalty and cooperation. In this chapter, you'll find ways of making conversation one of your best professional tools.

Constructive Conversation

You can relay things indirectly in conversation that you hesitate to say directly. To someone who interrupts you constantly at work, you could say: "I took some work home last night, and our oldest child interrupted me at least every two minutes. I simply can't concentrate when I'm interrupted. I said to Ellie, 'Look, honey, when I'm leaning over papers like this, it hurts to be interrupted.'" If the person doesn't take the hint, the next time they interrupt you, you can say, "Oh, no, you're worse than Ellie!"

Workplace conversations, especially between those who don't often associate, can help soften inelastic divisions between workers and departments. They provide a feeling of cooperation and sense of belonging to more than their small corner of the industry.

Allowing or encouraging casual exchanges among employees or co-workers can sometimes bring unexpected rewards in terms of the creation of new or better ideas. At the very least, sharing ideas in the nonthreatening, nondemanding atmosphere of an informal conversation sends all parties back to their drawing boards refreshed and inspired.

In an ideal world, people working on similar projects or in adjacent areas would have time for this kind of idea-sharing. In the real world, schedules and deadlines preempt it or schedule it in the form of meetings. It's sometimes the laid-back and completely unstructured talk that brings ideas to the fore.

> *As organizations grow and become more complex, they also tend to increase in rigidity. It becomes difficult to communicate with individuals both up and down as well as across the organizational structure. Levels of supervision, status, role distinction, technical training, multiple shifts, and the predictable differences of viewpoint between labor and management all cause problems in interpersonal communication.*
> —HAROLD P. ZELKO AND FRANK E.X. DANCE

Brief conversations in the hall, before meetings, on the way to the parking lot at night, and at whatever constitutes "the water cooler" for you can be a good way to make points that you don't want to magnify by sending a memo or by requesting a meeting. Offhand remarks can convey expectations you have of co-workers, supervisors, and staff members. You can also use casual remarks to build community, to foster interdepartmental ties, and to show each person they are recognized as an individual. You can indirectly smooth feelings that might have been ruffled in a recent meeting or mend fences over mild disagreements.

> *It is impossible to overrate the idea-producing power of conversation. ... some of the shrewdest business deals are those arranged over the luncheon table; some of the greatest scientific discoveries have come out of informal chats at annual meetings.*
> —RUDOLF FLESCH

> *The marvelous thing about good conversation is that it brings to birth so many half-realized thoughts of our own—besides sowing the seeds of innumerable other thought-plants.*
> —DAVID GRAYSON

If you are a manager, the brief conversations that you have throughout the workday give you a chance to take the communal pulse, to pick up on problems before they really are problems, to spot the employee who needs a pick-me-up or who is on the wrong track.

You pass someone in the hall and say, "How goes it?" They respond with a shrug, eyes sliding sideways, and a mumbled, "Fine." You reverse, and set up a meeting with the person in which you can probe for a problem in the making.

Another person might respond belligerently, "I'm doing the best I can." Meeting time. These are clues you might not come across until too late if it weren't for the small exchanges of conversation.

When you see an employee who usually dresses too casually for the job all decked out in a suit, you can say, "Hey, you look great! If you keep that up, you'll be running the place!" This is better than sending a reprimand memo. It might take a little longer for the point to be taken, but you will have preserved harmony and good feelings along the way.

An unhappy employee who's been overheard criticizing the company—or you—or who has received a reprimand might feel supported and accepted by a few minutes' conversation with someone who acknowledges their strong points. If you bring such a person in to discuss "attitude," you meet in a fairly unproductive gray area. The other person will most likely become defensive and little can be proved, so both parties leave feeling ruffled. Try conversing casually and positively instead.

Employees who appear to be wilting from lack of self-confidence can stand up straighter under the sun of a little light conversational approval and friendliness.

> *To pretend that people automatically know their value only brings on low morale and frustration in the work environment. Not only do people want to feel that what they're doing is important, they want to know that their efforts are appreciated.*
> —RICK PITINO

You can double the effects of your compliment if you deliver it in front of others, being careful of course not to be focusing on one person while no one else gets noticed. Some managers make a point of passing on a compliment by putting it in a memo and circulating it. For criticisms, they use the phone.

If you're alert to the nuances of your brief conversations, you can spot the longtime employee who is losing interest in the job, the one who is building resentment after being turned down for a raise or a promotion, and the individual seething over a rare bad decision or performance evaluation.

The work of dealing with these issues goes beyond mere conversation, but it is conversation that will point you in the right direction.

Increase the time you spend in casual conversation after a bout of companywide policy changes. Employees are destabilized, feeling uncertain and vulnerable, and a warm word can do wonders to restore the ground to pre-quake solidity.

People will rise to your expectations. What you convey to them in conversations tells them that you are impressed with their abilities and that you believe they will go far. They will try not to prove you wrong.

As an employee, you can use casual exchanges to convey problems or concerns to your supervisor without putting them on paper and you on the record: "How's it going?" "Great. Great. Although...there's not a lot of enthusiasm in the department for the new regulations."

> *Mastering small talk skills is more important in today's business environment than ever before.*
> —ANNE BABER AND LYNNE WAYMON

You might also be able to convey team-building feelings to co-workers without appearing patronizing: "Everyone is relieved that you managed to pull our bacon out of the fire;" "Was I ever excited when I saw what you'd come up with." (Patronizing would be, to a co-worker, "You did a nice job on that, Evan," as though you were evaluating him.)

Destructive Conversation

Destructive conversation consists of complaints and criticisms about the company, gossip and negative reflections on co-workers, and expressions of job dissatisfaction and hopes of moving on. One such person might simply be a malcontent and might indeed not appear some Monday morning. But when that person finds a sympathizer and they spread their unpleasantness, it can affect an entire department or company.

Workplace inequities, dangers, and illegalities are something else again. In that case, don't agonize, organize.

As an employee, it's up to you to foster the kind of conversation that moves your company forward and upward. If you are a manager, it behooves you to discuss this negativism with the employees involved. If a co-worker begins this sort of talk, you might either excuse yourself (interrupting the other person, if you must) or say something like: "I'm not sure I agree with you. Maybe we could talk about this some other time." Later, you could do a service to everyone by having a cup of coffee with the person to see what's behind the complaining.

Do's

▶ Keep conversations brief and superficial unless it has a work component. Time is money, and your time belongs to the people who pay you the money.

▶ If possible, include a word of appreciation in every conversation (see Chapter 2 for examples). You cannot mention often enough how much you appreciated the overtime your staff put in, or the many compliments you're getting from clients, or how deserved a recent promotion was. Don't worry about repeating yourself. Pats on the back are always accepted with delight.

It's worth your time to keep track of other people's

> *I yield to no one in my admiration for the office as a social center, but it's no place actually to get any work done.*
> —KATHARINE WHITEHORN

small and large successes so that when you run into them, you don't have to search for something to admire. A culture of mutual appreciation in the workplace can produce wonders of increased productivity, company loyalty, and fruitful energy.

An effective communication style can help you attain success in any career.
—Connie Podesta and Jean Gatz

In addition, although no one likes to anticipate trouble, people who have been appreciated are less likely to be belligerent and, when conflict arises, are more amenable to negotiation. Take the long view and make allies for the future—but with genuine kindness and interest, not self-serving flattery. The difference is clear to most people. If you cultivate an attitude that everyone you meet is doing their best (whether it seems like it or not to you) and that they want what we all want—happiness, health, a few nice surprises along the way—you can deliver your upbeat remarks with confidence and success.

▶ Talk with those who work under you the same way you'd like your superior to speak with you. This is not as easy as it sounds, so you will need to take your managerial temperature now and then to see if your attitude is producing resistance or if it is yielding increased efficiency and morale.

Small talk is essential to creating and enriching business relationships. Always begin and end your business conversation with small talk to humanize the relationship.
—Debra Fine

▶ Find common ground between you and the other person and emphasize areas of agreement. In work discussions, you will sometimes need to express divergent views. In casual conversations, however, it is more important to emphasize how you and the other person are alike. You could discuss nonconfidential work matters, extracurricular company activities, or shared interests outside work.

▶ Pay special attention to newcomers. They need a sense of acceptance and belonging more than the rest of us. You might say:

"If I can help you with anything, let me know."

"I hope you'll make yourself at home here."

"I'm delighted to meet you."

"In my opinion, you've made a terrific choice."

"It's a pleasure to have you join us."

"Let me know how I can help you feel at home more quickly."

"This is a good place to pitch your tent."

"Welcome aboard."

"Welcome to the team."

"When you have time, stop by and I'll introduce you to the people in my department."

> *There is probably no substitute for creating a culture—a set of attitudes, customs and habits throughout the organization—that favors easy two-way communication, in and out of channels, among all layers of the organization. Two key messages should be implicit in such a culture; (1) "You will know what's going on," and (2) "Your voice will be heard."*
>
> —JOHN W. GARDNER

Don'ts

▶ Don't be a naysayer. Not only does it make everyone feel small, it's not a good way of generating creative ideas. Assume that people will find the downsides of their ideas (if there are any) soon enough. Criticizing and crying doom will not make you popular, nor is a negative attitude likely to help you invent new ways of doing things. Discussing the problematic factors in work-related issues is helpful when you bring data, research, and well-thought-out arguments to the table. Simply objecting routinely to every new idea is not productive. In case you don't recognize a naysayer, this is the way one talks:

"I don't like it."

"I don't see it working."

"I don't think so."

"If you want to try it [sigh], go ahead, but I don't give much for your chances."

"It'll take too much time."

"It's up to you, of course, but personally..."

"It will cost way too much."

"It won't work. It just won't work."

"Nobody'll go for it."

"Oh, right, like that can be done."

"Someone's going to get hurt."

"Sure, like the brass is going to pay for it."

"That'll never happen."

"That's already been done."

"The whole thing is based on a false assumption."

"You call that innovation?"

"You might think that's a new approach, but let me tell you…"

▶ Don't use words and phrases that carry negative implications. Although almost any words, when strung together in the right order, could annoy a person, some are immediately inflammatory. For example, "But it's obvious" or "There's clearly a problem here" or "The answer is staring you right in the face." If the situation were truly obvious or clear, the other person would have seen it. Are you implying they're stupid? You are. And they know it.

▶ Avoid phrases like "you appear to think," "according to you," "you claim," and "if you are to be believed" (these imply that the other person speaks falsely). In the same way, "you must agree" or "at least you will admit" make the other person not want to agree or admit to anything. The only long-term way of dealing with words that say one thing and mean another is to become aware of your own speech and to watch other people's reactions to it. You'll soon realize which expressions bring a tight look to someone's face and which bring a smile.

▶ Don't bring up personal issues unless they are truly relevant to the business being discussed. Some companies foster a family-type culture where everyone knows everyone's personal business. If this is an entrenched, firm-wide custom, you will need to go along with it. In general, however, personal agendas don't belong in the workplace.

▶ Avoid discussing sensitive or controversial work issues (possible layoffs, unacceptable work by someone, rumors about a new hire). This sort of talk will always return to your doorstep. It should be reserved for the one or two

Employees are not your family, or even your friends. Don't drag personal emotions or relationships into the business situation.
—JANE WESMAN

co-workers who are also good friends, and it should take place off site.
- Avoid casual conversations completely if you work in the front office, in the reception room, or in any area where customers and clients are welcomed. Chatting employees create a negative impression.

In retail sales, it is understandable that when there is truly nothing to do, salespeople may chat with each other. The big no-no is not stopping the conversation instantly—and that means in midsentence or even midword—when a customer approaches.

Special Situations

- People who'd rather talk than work are not a problem for you as long as they talk to themselves. If they're talking to you, however, they pose two problems: (1) you will become annoyed because you can't get your work done and (2) you might undeservedly share the blame for talking when you should be working. Try saying something like:

"Hey, just in time! Can you run these boxes down to the mailroom for me?"

"I absolutely don't have a second."

"I really can't stop now. This was supposed to be finished yesterday." (Then return to your work whether the other person leaves or stays to say, "This will only take a minute.")

"Later, 'gator. This has got to go out today."

"No, no, not now, Will. Can't talk." (Return to work.)

"Oh good. Leo next door was looking for someone to help stuff the mailers. I'll tell him you're free."

"Oops! Bad timing. I am so not free!"

"Say, if you don't have anything to do, you could take care of the recycling today. I don't have time myself."

"Seeing you reminds me I've got to call over to Human Resources. (Pick up phone. Dial anything.) May I speak with you later?"

"You'll have to come back later, OK? I'm drowning in work."

Occasionally, a particularly dense person will ignore even blatant commands to "Go away!" You might need to say: "Look, Jean, I am incapable of chatting at work. It makes me too nervous. I'm on Maalox now, and I think it's the interruptions that are doing it.

We're going to have to get together outside work because stopping to talk like this is literally making me ill." And then do not discuss it. Keep repeating, "I'm sorry but I won't be able to chat with you at work anymore. I'm sorry but I won't be able to chat with you at work anymore."

▶ Whether it's the CEO of a billion-dollar company or your immediate manager, talking with someone above you in the workplace hierarchy is often fraught with trepidation. Your attitude should be one of respect, but not of slack-jawed awe, of confidence but not of overfamiliarity.

Begin by addressing the person with full name and title. Wait to be invited to call them by their first name. Let the other person lead the conversation. Only add something original or on a different subject if you seem to be left an opening for it. Let the other person decide when the conversation is over. These signals of the pecking order are subtle, but real.

▶ If you are aware that an employee or a co-worker is in treatment for substance abuse or is returning to work after rehabilitation, you might acknowledge the situation by saying something like, "Good luck with everything. If you need anything, let me know. And congratulations on making it through treatment." If you think it appropriate, assure them that you will not be mentioning their situation to anyone.

▶ When a co-worker suffers the death of a family member, you will want to say something. Saying anything—no matter how awkward you might think you are—is far, far better than saying nothing. The person will long remember your thoughtfulness but will never be able to recall your exact words.

▶ Jokes can create a pleasant atmosphere in a short time. However, jokes must be carefully chosen and cannot be off-color or bigoted. Even if your joke about a certain ethnic group or featuring four-letter words brings down the house, others will think a little less of you for passing on something inappropriate to the workplace (see Chapter 6 on how and when to tell jokes).

Topics of Conversation

There are obviously exceptions to every guideline, so use your own antennae to determine what topics are suitable for your workplace and for the people with whom you're talking at the moment.

The guiding principle about workplace conversations is that no one is being paid to shoot the breeze. Unlike conversations at social events, where you are relaxed and can idly talk about many topics, workplace conversations are primarily a bridge, a link, a way to pleasantly segue from one piece of work to the next.

If you pass someone in the hall, it is much friendlier to exchange a few words. If you're waiting in an outer office to see someone, it is natural to strike up a brief conversation with anyone else who's there. As you arrive in the morning or leave in the evening, you often converse with whoever's going your way.

Work conversations often take place on the fly, as you're walking, waiting, or busy doing something with your hands. Numerous small moments in the workday allow for friendly exchanges. This is really what is meant by "small talk." Discussions about the work itself are in another category (they're sometimes called "meetings").

Most general topics lend themselves to this sort of small talk in the workplace. An exception is talking politics. Naturally, we all have freedom of speech, but water-cooler talk about political issues is, firstly, a distraction from work, and secondly, a source of potential conflict and ill-feeling that creates an officewide sense of uneasiness.

Those in positions of authority need to avoid expressing their own political preferences, as this places undue pressure on employees. Some civic-minded companies encourage their employees to vote. Others give them a day or half-day off to go to the polls. Still others go further, showing partisanship by means of a corporate decision to support a certain candidate or issue. This makes it difficult for employees who do not agree with the company's choices. It's best to keep politics out of the workplace.

Topics to Consider

Anecdotes, opinions, observations

Books and movies: recent movie or book you recommend, what the other has seen or read lately

Fitness: noontime run or walk, invitation to try out a nearby gym, current fitness news, the new and more healthful cafeteria offerings

Hobbies: how you keep rabbits from eating your garden; asking if the other person has any interest in genealogy, building a kayak, or joining a quilting club

Local interest: restaurant you recommend or want to know about; asking for a recommendation of a realtor, barber, or beauty salon;

discussing a current community theater production or the new stop signs being installed

Newspaper (but no politics or controversial issues): odd reports, news about the community, cartoon strip

Sports: recent game, sports figure in the news, upcoming match, predictions for the World Series or other big event, the company-sponsored golf tournament

Surroundings: traffic or parking problems, building renovations or changes, practical questions about new company policies

Weather: record-setting high or low temperatures and how they affected your car this morning, your garden yesterday, your sleep last night; a brief factoid about weather; a memory about weather

Topics to Avoid

Complaints of any sort

Confidential matters, even if you think the person you're speaking with knows about them

The importance of discretion increases with closeness to the top of a hierarchical organization.
—Rosabeth Moss Kanter

Criticisms of other people in the company or of the company culture

Gossip or discussions of co-workers

Intrusive questions about the other person

Lascivious talk about other employees

Politics, religion, sex, and controversial civic issues

Put-downs of people you work with

Salaries—yours or other people's

Something you "put over" on your boss

Your opinions about what the company/your boss is doing wrong, even when you know the others are sympathetic to your views

Your own work failures, problems, shortcomings

Your personal affairs: family, health, problems

Your plans to move on from this company eventually

Conversation Starters

"Any plans for the weekend?"

"Any predictions for the game tonight?"

"Are you a Knicks fan?"

"Are you going to the regatta this weekend?"

"Did you get the bear today or did the bear get you?"

"Did you have trouble with the e-mail system today?"

"Do you have much of a commute?"

"Have you always lived in this area?"

"Have you worked here long?"

"Hey, what's up?"

"Hi, Gina! I had a note today from the protocol office that I thought you'd be interested in. I'll send it over tomorrow."

"Hi! How's it going?"

"How did you know to bring an umbrella today?"

"How's life treating you?"

"How was your day today?"

"How was your vacation?"

"I noticed you've got ski racks on your car—where do you usually ski?"

"I see you often, but I don't think we've been introduced. My name is Farley Winsome."

"I've been meaning to ask you if you ever found someone to replace your assistant."

"Say, I heard that your patent application went through. Congratulations!"

"This is my first week here. Could you tell me if there's a gym nearby?"

"What do you think about the new parking arrangements?"

"Working late?"

If They Say...You Say

In many types of conversation, your response is intended to keep the conversation going. They say something, you say something and then add a question so that the ball is back in their court. In the workplace, the idea is not to prolong a conversation, so your back-and-forthing is a little drier, meant only to assure the other person of your goodwill. If a conversation reveals something that needs to be discussed, take it to the next level and schedule a meeting with the other person.

If They Say	You Say
"I just turned in my project."	"That's great! You worked hard. You must be relieved to be finished."
"Things are going okay. I guess."	"Why don't you come to my office around 2? It's been too long since we've had a chat."
"Hey, how's it going?"	"I can't complain. How about you?"
"Congratulations on meeting the Grismley deadline."	"Nice of you to mention it! We're pretty pleased. It was a near thing at times."
"You know who bugs me? Denny bugs me."	"Denny? He always says such nice things about you. I kinda like the guy. Oh, hey, I've got to run. See you tomorrow!"
"I'm worried about this new contract."	"I am too. Why don't we call upstairs and see if we can talk with Hank?"
"So how's your love life?"	"If you don't mind, I never talk about it."
"I hate to go home when it's raining like this. The whole family's going to be in the house and the kids'll be fighting."	"Really." [flatly]

Closing Lines

In a business environment, conversation is rarely lengthy, and the same is true of last remarks:

"Call me tomorrow."

"Congratulations again on your promotion—everyone is so pleased for you."

"Give me a call next week, will you? Here's my card."

"Good luck with the new project."

"I'll ask Frederica to call you with the information."

"I'll get back to you next week."

"I'll see you at the next meeting."

"It was good having a few minutes with you."

"Let me know how it turns out."

"More on this later."

"See you next week."

"Take care now."

"Take it easy!"

CHAPTER 10

Talking With Anyone at Meetings and Conferences

> *I wonder how many of our tombstones will have to be inscribed with the epitaph "Died of too many Meetings"?*
> —HANNAH WHITALL SMITH (1891)

Introduction

Every day, around the world, millions and millions of meetings take place. Does that give you a little perspective on the three (only three!) meetings you have scheduled today?

Valuable work gets done not just in meetings, but in the seemingly casual conversations that spring up before and after workshops, seminars, meetings, symposia, and conferences—and during the breaks, too.

It's easier to be noticed when you're chatting one-on-one with someone than it is to stand out in a meeting or conference largely dominated by others. You can also express opinions or impress people with your intelligence and ideas in small groups of two, three, or four more memorably than you can while others are speaking or while an agenda is being rigorously pursued.

For success in any meeting, you'll want to look alert, listen attentively, and be prepared to ask a good question or make an impressive contribution to the conversation. If you aren't adding something useful, it's better to say nothing and look wise.

The best way to appear confident and poised is to actually believe that you are competent and that you can handle anything that comes your

> *The effort required to make favorable first impression is less than the effort required to undo an unfavorable one.*
> —D.A. BENTON

way. It's disillusioning but true that the appearance of being competent is almost as good in today's world as actually being competent. Naturally, it is to be hoped that you are both. But the essential is to believe you are capable.

The worst thing you can do is to mull over and hug to yourself previous gaffes and awkwardnesses. Going into new conversations with that kind of baggage is a way of shooting yourself in the foot.

You've made mistakes, you've turned in work that was less than perfect, you've misspoken a few times. But so have we all. Forget about your faux pas (assuming that you've already resolved not to repeat them), and head into the next meeting with confidence.

No matter what kind of a meeting it is—planning, presentation, evaluation, decision making, problem solving—it isn't always strictly business. The little remarks that get tossed out, the one-liners, the spontaneous chatter after a surprising announcement, the mutterings and asides of unhappy campers all affect the meeting for better or for worse. You want to see that it's for better.

At in-house meetings you'll know or at least be familiar with the other attendees. At conferences, conventions, and workshops, there might be a few people from your company, but most will be strangers. Your conversation will vary depending on whether you're meeting someone for the first time or if you already know them.

> *The length of a meeting rises with the number of people present and the productiveness of a meeting falls with the square of the number of people present.*
> —EILEEN SHANAHAN

If you're planning a meeting or conference, leave small blocks of time for conversation. Much can be done in these short periods: encouraging those who can't get a word in edgewise, forestalling your resident critic, asking for support, letting idea people know that they can push the envelope if they like.

Too many meetings and conferences are planned right down to the minute—and this is usually sensible and cost-efficient. However, try to leave some room for the unexpected, the serendipitous, the offbeat. Conversing in an unstructured way before a meeting is stimulating and empowering—and provides a nice contrast for the structure of the meeting that follows.

Do's

▶ The most successful meetings are those in which participants take some ownership. Whether you are planning the meeting or going to it, strive for a sense that the meeting is important to you, and you to it. Use the time before meetings to foster this attitude. Have as many people as possible help plan, set up, and run the meeting. The conversations along the way can be gently steered in an upbeat direction. When you have people who are making the meeting happen, the meeting becomes a happening event.

▶ Use those few minutes before a meeting or conference while people are pouring coffee and getting settled to conduct an informal poll: "What would you like to see happen in the meeting this morning?" "What do you think our real problem is?" If you are helping to run the meeting, this will give you some insight into people's thoughts.

▶ If you know who your reserved people are—the ones who have a hard time getting heard or those who fear ending up chopped liver if they say anything—spend a few minutes with them and sprinkle a few words of encouragement into the conversation. You might mention—if this is true—that the conference or meeting organizers are determined to keep things positive. Those who have a criticism will fill out an evaluation form afterwards. In addition, facilitators are going to call on people, not only respond to those who take over the floor.

▶ You can forestall problems you've had at previous conferences or meetings by a word to the wise. If one of your group interrupts constantly, the place to deal with it might be in small, informal conversations in the hall.

The first time they interrupt, say something like, "Whoa, Marcus, let Sweeney finish what he was saying." If you do this several times at widely spaced intervals, when

> *I learned that in dealing with things, you spent much more time and energy in dealing with people than in dealing with things.*
> —BUWEI YANG CHAO

the behavior crops up in a meeting, you have a history for saying lightly, "Marcus, are you at it again?"

It will sound friendly, like in-group knowledge, but there will be enough embarrassment on Marcus's part to possibly effect a cure. Use the same strategy with those who are always hurrying others along, finishing their sentences, and acting impatient.

Before a meeting is also a good time to have a brief chat with your chronic busybody. Somewhere in the conversation, mention how distracting comings and goings are to the rest of the group.

With those who control a meeting with their unrelenting talk, drowning out others and dominating the direction of the discussion, you can start small in a group conversation days before the meeting: "Beverly, you've got quite a bit to say there. I did want to hear from Gene, though." Calling someone into your office to talk about this habit might make the issue seem bigger than it is. On the other hand, sometimes an ounce of prevention can head people off at the pass, mixed metaphors aside. In the meeting, when the person starts taking over again, you can say something similar but by now the sting is gone.

> *Loudmouths are a common breed, gravitating naturally to meetings of all kinds.*
> —MICHAEL DOYLE AND DAVID STRAUS

To a more hardened case, you might say something indirect like, "Have you noticed that Robin and Dean and Fitz rarely speak up in meetings? How could they be encouraged to contribute more?" "I feel that we aren't hearing from everyone in these meetings. What would you think about asking everyone to offer at least one idea?" "I wonder if should set a time limit for each person. I'd like to hear more from some of those who never get to talk."

▶ Before you head into the meeting, turn off your cell phone. In most offices it isn't necessary, but if you've had problems before, you might start the meeting by saying: "Please turn off all cell phones or set them to vibrate."

▶ If you're helping to plan or run a meeting or conference, you'd do well to consider how the few minutes before the meeting can enhance your goals for the meeting. Having plenty of coffee and refreshments will keep people cheerful and hydrated. See that attendees know they will have a few minutes to chat with each other before going in. If they don't know that, they hesitate to start a conversation—and it could be a useful exchange.

> *You'd better answer that. It could be someone important.*
> —QUEEN ELIZABETH II, TO A WOMAN WHOSE CELL PHONE RANG DURING A FORMAL MEETING

▶ In the same way, plan for post-meeting atmosphere or activities to solidify what you accomplished in the meeting. See what you can find out by mingling: How did you think the meeting went? Did you leave dissatisfied? Why? What decisions got made that pleased you? What was unexpected about the meeting—anything?

You can always pass out evaluations, but what you pick up in a relaxed conversation after a meeting might be more valuable.

When meetings don't go well, people take their frustrations back with them to their desks or work stations. There is actually considerable time lost after ineffective meetings and attendees are said to be suffering from meeting recovery syndrome. One of the keys to employee productivity, creativity, efficiency, participation, and commitment is the effective meeting. And conversation before and after meetings and conferences will give you some excellent pointers on making the next meeting even better.

▶ The business culture is not very forgiving of errors, mishaps, ignorance, and snafus—the public ones, at any rate. This makes it hard for anyone to admit that they're stumped.

In connection with meetings and conferences, you might find yourself mortified that you don't know the answer to a question. Remember that to most people, this is nothing. If you react with horror, consternation, or embarrassment when something goes awry, it will only emphasize your helplessness.

Instead, say something like, "I don't know the answer to that. But I'll look into it and get back to you." Or: "I'm not sure what went wrong. But it won't happen again." If you always follow through on your promises, people will trust you—and they'll trust you more than the person who claims to be perfect or to have all the answers. Meetings and conferences are embarrassingly public places to appear in the wrong, but if you carry it off calmly, few people will remember.

▶ In brief conversations before a meeting, generate good feelings. Making other people look good makes you look good too. Before you offer a compliment, think about the difference between fawning, sycophantic remarks and appreciative remarks that are both true and simple (that is, not gushy).

Few human beings are proof against the implied flattery of rapt attention.
—JACK WOODFORD

If you can't think of anything that works, ask a question about the other person's topic. A good question—followed by giving them your whole attention—shows that you value what they're saying.

Other ways of showing your appreciation of people is to introduce them to those they don't know. The implication is that you are proud to introduce them to your acquaintances. You can also bring them into the conversation and show that you were listening to them by saying something like, "Jake, you said the same thing a minute ago."

▶ The few unstructured minutes before and after meetings and conferences allow you to pick up valuable information about staff morale, attitudes, and interpersonal relations. Note who gravitates to whom, who is left out of groups, which groups seem upbeat and content, which groups wear frowns and appear to be complaining. These small blocks of free time allow employees to revert to a more casual level of relating to each other, a level that can be instructive to those who are aware of the group dynamics.

> *The office grapevine is 75% to 95% accurate and provides managers and staff with better information than formal communications, according to a recent study. Rather than ignore or try to repress the grapevine, it's crucial for executives to tune into it.*
>
> —CAROL HYMOWITZ

Don'ts

▶ Resist the temptation to talk about your professional or technical ideas with others while you're standing around waiting for a meeting to begin. You are not on record at that point, and your idea might lodge in someone else's head, someone who conveniently forgets it isn't theirs.

Some people are good at putting two and two together, especially when one of the twos belongs to someone else. Coincidentally, these people seem more aggressive and outgoing than the people who actually have the ideas, so they're more likely to brazen through in a public forum with "their" ideas. And once an idea is presented in a meeting, it's forever associated with the person who brought it up.

> *The most likely place to have your idea-pocket picked is at a meeting. ... Here an idea becomes public property the moment it hits the air waves.*
>
> —JANE TRAHEY

Other people truly don't remember where they heard an idea, but because it shows up in their head, they assume it's theirs. They would be astonished if you told them the idea wasn't original with them. Quite truly, innocently astonished.

The workplace has areas where brainstorming, sharing of ideas, and collegiality are appropriate and necessary. Telling someone outside your department about an idea that's new to them or that you haven't told anyone else about is not a good idea. Wait until you're in the meeting and can present your idea on the record.

▶ Don't complain about the number, kind, planning, or running of meetings and conferences. At least not before or after an actual meeting. Complain later, when you are far away from the group attending the meeting. It's too easy to be overheard and get labeled as a malcontent. Many people dislike attending meetings, but it doesn't help anyone to say so, and it makes you look whiny compared to those who are biting their tongues to keep from saying what you said.

▶ Don't talk just to be talking. It's better to remain quiet and look as though you know lots of things than to say something that proves you don't. You will be charged more heavily for saying something inane than for saying nothing at all. On the other hand, make an effort to contribute at least one useful or memorable comment to any conversation.

> *If you can't add to the discussion, don't subtract by talking.*
> —LOIS WYSE

▶ While waiting for a meeting to start or while dispersing slowly afterwards, don't join the same people you work with all day or the people you're most comfortable with. Mingle. This is a chance to meet other people and schmooze with managers you don't normally see.

Out of general graciousness, speak with those who might never be able to give you a raise or a promotion or help you with your work. What goes around comes around, and although those people might not repay your attention, other people will. In addition, it's the right thing to do.

Special Situations

▶ When attending conferences, conventions, and workshops that include people from other companies, you'll want to be especially vigilant not to speak of confidential matters and to always give a positive view of your company. To make conversation, you might say something like:

"Are you familiar with the book written by our last speaker?"

"Are you hoping to get something specific from the conference?"

"Do you attend every year?"

"Do you know if you can get an extra syllabus somewhere?"

"Do you know many of these people?"

"Have you attended this convention before?"

"Have you been doing any sightseeing while you're here?"

"Have you been in this industry all your life?"

"Have you ever heard this next speaker?"

"How long have you been working for Fieldings?"

"How many people from your group are attending?"

"I'm not familiar with your company. Will you give me a little background?"

"Say, there's an excellent restaurant within walking distance I'm telling everyone about it because it's really a find."

"Someone asked me the other day what advice I'd give to someone new in this field, and I've been thinking about it ever since. Do you have any ideas?"

"What attracted you to this line of work?"

"What is your company's vision?"

"What part of the conference are you most interested in?"

"Where do you call home?"

▶ Most people who want to keep their jobs today know better than to get into noisy arguments or sly, persistent feuds with co-workers or managers. On the other hand, some people don't know better.

If you can catch these mismatches in human chemistry before they blow up your department, you can save yourself the trouble of putting the pieces together later.

You can always try bringing the two into your office for a discussion of their antagonisms, but it might not be effective. Like Dorothy Walworth's couple, they might bury the hatchet, but in a shallow, well-marked grave.

You can also order, insist, and demand that they cease and desist. But this kind of force doesn't get at

The only way to get the best of an argument is to avoid it.
—DALE CARNEGIE

the core problem. And, as Deborah Tannen points out, "Smashing heads does not open minds."

Low-key, private conversations with each allow you to show general goodwill and provide a friendly context for the subject, which you could disguise a little. You might mention the unfortunate results a few years ago when two employees—now ex-employees—couldn't seem to get along. Or you could relay Ann Landers' observation (to each of them) that "it takes two to make an argument. The one who is wrong is the one who will be doing most of the talking."

Remember, too, the supreme value of good questions. Without sounding accusatory, try to get them to tell you their feelings and thoughts and issues with their adversary. It's amazing but true that sometimes all a person needs is to be thoroughly listened to in order to get beyond something they're stuck on.

Topics of Conversation

Conversations in these situations—before and after business gatherings—are necessarily short and choppy. You don't know when things are going to turn businesslike and cut you off in the middle of a sentence. Because of that, topics like your vacation or the other person's or your hobby or theirs don't really work. This is a special kind of communication where superficial sentences are traded until it's time to go in. However, don't undervalue their effect on others. Those who operate well in this situation gain points with others, especially their superiors.

Topics to Consider

Anecdotes, opinions, observations

Books, movies, TV shows

Current news, if noncontroversial

Holidays

New software: virtues and drawbacks

Quick thoughts about: solar energy, space travel, the arts

Refreshments being served

Setting: good choice of venue, better than last year

Sports

Weather: glad to be inside, wish they were outside

If enough meetings are held, the meetings become more important than the problem.
—SUSAN OHANIAN

Topics to Avoid

Blatantly pushing for raise or promotion

Bragging

Comments about others in attendance—their looks, their behavior, their work

Complaints about work, hours, pay

Confidential matters

Controversial issues

Criticisms of co-workers, the company, the management

Domestic complaints or revelations

Illnesses

Long stories

Money

Networking too obviously and aggressively

Off-color jokes

Personal problems, foibles, failures, divorces

Politics

Religion

Salaries

Sex

Your children or grandchildren

> *Any committee is only as good as the most knowledgeable, determined and vigorous person on it. There must be somebody who provides the flame.*
> —LADY BIRD JOHNSON

Conversation Starters

"Are you enjoying your stay?"

"Are you feeling any optimism about the stock market?"

"Excuse me, have you taken the workshop on privacy issues?"

"Hi, come join us. We were trying to decide the most significant challenges that U.S. business faces today."

"Hi! Did you hear that last announcement? I missed it."

"Hi. I'm Donald Condon from Heavy Metals. I don't think I know you."

"Hi. I'm Sharyn Larson, and I don't know a single soul here. Do you?"

"How has the Internet affected you, professionally speaking?"

"How's the economy affecting you over at Weisen and Raine?"

"How was your vacation?"

"Is anyone sitting here? Thanks. I'm Robert Conway from Abel's."

"I see in the paper that your daughter made the Dean's list. Congratulations to her!"

"I see you here and there in the halls, but I don't think we've met. My name is Jessica Flinders."

"Lillian! Just the person I wanted to see. I'm thinking of taking a ballet class. Where would you recommend I start?"

"Mike! I thought of you when I was watching the Red Sox game last night—you must be over the moon!"

"Say, did you attend this last session—what did you think about the panel's conclusion?"

"This is the most perfect fall day. For some reason I always think fall is best spent on a college campus, and here we are, on a beautiful one. Did you ever feel that connection?"

"Were you at the conference last year?"

If They Say...You Say

It takes a bit of juggling to hold a conversation that may be interrupted any moment, so you want to keep it light, casual, and cursory—just, perhaps, this side of inane. You show your goodwill, you trade industry talk, and you keep a lookout for a person or an idea you might be interested in.

If They Say	You Say
"Does it seem to you that this convention rolls around more than once a year?"	"I'll say! Where does the time go? Have you taken any trips since last year?"
"I'm starting a group to work on science projects with fourth graders in an after-school program. Are any of you interested?"	"Tell you what, I'm pretty busy at the moment, but here's my card—give me a call sometime and you can tell me more about it."

Talking With Anyone at Meetings and Conferences

"Hey, I got a great joke about a Polack, a Jew, an Eyetie, and a Mick."

"Charlie? Charlie? I don't think so."

"Hello. I'm Sammie Winston, and you look awfully familiar to me."

"There's a reason for that. I'm Jules Thierry, and about six years ago we and two other families carpooled together. But of course the drivers rarely ran into each other, so to speak."

"Say, did you hear about the trouble Lowell is in?"

"That reminds me. I've got to see if my son needs a ride home from practice."

"Shirley, why don't you be a good girl and get us all some coffee?"

"Van, did you know that a girl is usually no older than thirteen to sixteen, tops? And, um, have you been living in a cave or something for the past twenty years?"

"I remember you from last year! You gave that talk on home studies. That was terrific!"

"Actually, I wasn't here last year but that's okay, I thought for a minute you were my brother-in-law whom I haven't seen in ten years."

Closing Lines

Because every conversation stops automatically when the meeting or conference begins or when people head for home or office, you don't have to end your chat as graciously or as tactfully as you might in another setting. Brief and friendly will do it:

"Back to the salt mines."

"Bye!"

"Don't work too hard."

"Give my best to your family."

"Good luck with that project—sounds terrific."

"Have a good one!"

"I enjoyed talking with you."

"It's good to catch up on your news."

"Let me know what you decide, will you?"

"Maybe I'll catch you after the dinner tonight."

"See you at the next one."

"Take care!"

"Tell Hank I said hello when you see him on Monday."

"Why do I like the breaks better than the sessions?"

CHAPTER 11

Talking With Anyone at Business-Social Events

> *Even though talking is something we do every day, there are lots of situations where it can be difficult and situations where we could do it better. The road to success, whether it's social or professional, is paved with talk.*
> —LARRY KING

Introduction

The line between business and social events is not always clear-cut: many businesses are involved with community affairs, fundraising committees, and charity drives. They often sponsor nonprofit organizations from the community, which in turn hold teas, picnics, dinners, and other social gatherings. Thus you might be invited to something ostensibly social—a club dinner, a bazaar, a ball—where the primary associations are work-related.

You want to relax because it's a social occasion, but you are aware that work colleagues will notice if you leave too much of your professional self behind. After one or two such events, you'll figure out how to be relaxed but not too relaxed.

> *Of indoor entertainments, the truest and most human is conversation.*
> —MARK PATTISON

Do's

▶ Even if (especially if) you are well known in this group, wear a name tag if everyone else is wearing one.

- Stand near the door. This allows you to speak with a number of people in a relatively short time.
- Attitude is everything. If you look friendly and approachable and if you both approach others and let them approach you, you will be a conversational success.
- Follow the classic pattern for good conversations: see that you hit the ball back over the net to the other person whenever it comes your way. This means your conversation consists partly of statements, some of which reveal a little of you to the other person, and partly of questions, to get the other person to reveal a little of themselves. Always relate your statement or your question to what has gone before.
- Because of the nature of a business-social event, you don't want to gravitate to a small group of workmates and talk shop, nor do you want to be entirely social, treating people as potential friends. The best way to be neither fish nor fowl is to choose neutral topics to talk about, to ask what the other person thinks about local changes or events, about national trends, about current popular culture, books, and movies. The daily newspaper usually has half a dozen topics that can be brought into a conversation to good effect. Steer clear of controversy, however.

> *Always read at least one paper a day, and know what's going on. It certainly isn't necessary to be an expert on the gold standard or the Supreme Court, but know enough so that you won't look completely blank when they're mentioned.*
> —HILDEGARDE DOLSON

- To respond to another person, you add to what they said, going in the same direction. Try not to contradict or object to what they're saying. Usually conversation at this type of event will be lighthearted so the content of what anyone says is not as important as the other person feeling heard and agreed with.
- Make your conversations "Yes, and..." not "Yes, but...". If someone says, "We should have invited another fifty people tonight," you say, "Yes, and that might have put us over the top of our fundraising goal," instead of saying, "Yes, but feeding that many more would probably have eaten up, you might say, anything they donated."

  Some people have a naturally argumentative nature, and they positively enjoy taking the contrary position on anything that's mentioned. Individuals with oppositional temperament are exhausting. If this is you, have your fun with close friends and family but spare social and business acquaintances.

- Include everyone in your group in the conversation. Watch for those who look as though they might have something to add but can't get a leg into the conversation. Give them an opening. If you manage to pass the talking baton to all those around you, they will leave convinced you are a brilliant conversationalist, and never mind that they can't remember exactly what you said.

> *The mark of good conversation is that every member of the company takes part in it, and that all discuss the same theme.*
> —JOHN ERKSINE

- Carry your beverage in your left hand. This leaves your right hand free for handshakes and ensures that your hand isn't damp and cold. Even if you are left-handed, tradition dictates that we shake hands with the right hand.

- Eat or talk. Doing both at the same time is not suave.

- Be mindful of the person or persons who accompanied you to the event. If they're from your private life, they won't be familiar with the business half of the room, and vice versa. Introduce them to people with whom they might have something in common. This also allows you to mingle.

- Be discreet. Even though co-workers are present, don't discuss matters that belong at work. And where, at a purely social event, you might relax and, as they used to say, let down your hair, this is not the place for it. People from your place of work are there and will notice any behavior that is too "relaxed."

- Talk slowly and quietly. At big, noisy events, people tend to raise their voices. Understandably so. However, if you want the undivided attention of your listeners, lower your voice a little—they will lean nearer—and speak slowly, pausing from time to time. Nothing quite holds people as much as an assured speaker—and that's what you'll look like, speaking slowly and only loudly enough to be heard.

- Be patient. The start-up costs of a conversation have to be paid by someone, and it might as well be you. Some people will be off and running as soon as you join them. Others need to be warmed up and brought along slowly. But it's often the latter who eventually hit their conversational stride and surprise you with special knowledge, a dry sense of humor, or a story that was worth waiting for.

Don'ts

▶ Don't bring your time-is-money business mind-set with you, even though the event is both business and social. You could end up with a series of five-second conversations:

"Hey!"

"How's it going?"

"Good. You?"

"Good."

"Great."

To avoid this Indy 500 pace, don't give or ask for one-word answers. Elaborate. Tell an anecdote. Ask a question that needs more than a "yes" or "no."

At its scintillating best, conversation is a social game in which all can join, and at which all can score. It is a game that requires neither courts, links, nor other equipment. It is always in season, and will be popular as long as civilization itself endures.

—LILLIAN EICHLER

▶ Don't use business jargon at a business-social event unless you're talking shop with one or two other people who are enjoying it as much as you are. Otherwise, leave the buzz words at work.

▶ This hybrid affair is social, but the business component means that you don't bring domestic situations into the discussion, unless you are speaking with one or two of your best friends or co-workers.

▶ By the same token, the social component of this hybrid affair means that you don't bring work to it. Work successes, problems, gossip, or news should wait for another time.

▶ Don't let your ego take over. Particularly if you are a business executive, accustomed to commanding people's attention and expecting their deference, you might carry this attitude over into the social arena, where it is less appreciated.

In an effort to find a topic, people sometimes pull out that which is dearest to them: a golf triumph, a grand slam at the bridge table, or some other business or extracurricular success. If told modestly and humorously, this makes for good conversation. If not, not.

- Don't blatantly network. All casual conversations at functions like these are in some ways a kind of networking, but asking for information, favors, interviews, references, or other business-related propositions is inappropriate at a social event, even if it is underwritten by the business community.

- Don't talk solely with people you know well. Make a point of meeting at least three new people. Try to find three things you have in common with each of them. This three-three strategy is not only good practice for your social skills, but it is an important stimulus to the goals of the event and might bring you unexpected personal and professional dividends in ways you couldn't possibly foresee at the moment.

- Don't overdo your enthusiasm for the purpose of the event or for the organizers or for the food and the site. You want people to know you appreciated their efforts, but a low-key, "Congratulations on pulling this together" or "Wonderful buffet!" will go a long way.

- Don't make any assumptions. Asking, "Are you married? Do you have kids?" can be awkward. Say instead, if you're at that point in the conversation where you are exchanging personal information, "Tell me about your family" or "Do you have family in the area?"

Special Situations

- A company banquet that honors outstanding contributions by employees during the past year is a perfect example of a business-social occasion. The only caveat here is that everyone who attends ought to act as though this is simply the best, most outstanding, most wonderful company in the world.

- If you're one of the organizers of a fundraiser or if you feel strongly about the purpose of the event, be as persistent as you are gracious in overtly or covertly appealing for financial support. People won't love you for this sort of thing, of course, but they expect it.

  In mingling with the guests, make ordinary small talk, mentioning something personal about everyone with whom you speak (if you can). But feel free to add such reminders as:

  "Have an extra piece of cake tonight! It's a small return on what you've done for the association."

  "How good of you to come tonight. It means a lot to us to know you support the foundation."

"I'd like to make a small toast to the five of you for being such special friends to the institute."

"Thank you for your wonderful support in the past. It looks as though you're going to continue to back the organization."

"We are so grateful to people like you. We know we can always count on you."

Topics of Conversation

In a business-social setting, where small talk is the order of the day, you will want to aim for noncontroversial subjects with general appeal.

Topics to Consider

Anecdotes, opinions, observations

Books: new, recently read

Cartoon strip

Concerts, musical groups

Favorite restaurants, coffee shops, delicatessens, bakeries

Hobbies, if there's a shared interest

Local-interest news or events

Movies: recently seen, favorite, one you or they have seen multiple times

Noncontroversial national events

Occasion: how it came about, if you or they are especially involved in organizing or supporting it

Sports: recent games, upcoming series games, favorite teams, players, local sports, sports you or they participate in

Surroundings, especially if they are unusual or you've never been there before, or if you have questions about them; good seating arrangements; attractive decor; too warm or too cold

The choice of a topic which will bear analysis and support enthusiasm, is essential to the enjoyment of conversation.
—Agnes Repplier

The arts: local theater, museums, arts you or they practice

Traffic, parking, rush hour, if it's not a complaint

Travel, if it is a back-and-forth conversation and not a lecture about your trip

Weather, especially if it's been record-setting or dramatic (fires, floods, tornadoes)

> *Too often travel, instead of broadening the mind, merely lengthens the conversation.*
> —ELIZABETH DREW

Topics to Avoid

An event to which others might not have been invited

Complaints about your company or other employees

Confidential matters, secrets, inside knowledge of any kind

Controversial subjects: abortion, capital punishment, assisted suicide, welfare system, affirmative action, political races, etc.

Criticisms of others, whether known or unknown to listeners

Death

Domestic complaints

Illnesses, health problems

Money: how much things cost, rising inflation, how much the fundraiser might garner tonight, high medical costs

Off-color jokes

Personal problems, shortcomings, feelings

Politics

Religion

Retelling the plots of movies, books, or TV shows

Salaries—yours or theirs

Sex

Work problems

Your children

Your divorce

Your love life

> *Politics and religion are dangerous subjects, for they may cause ill feeling even in the most cultivated company. Illness, death, and disaster are unpleasant, and consequently should be avoided.*
> —LILLIAN EICHLER

Conversation Starters

The first thing you do, of course, is extend your hand for a handshake while saying, "Hi! I'm Corky Johnson, and I'm with Arcoban." Unless it's a friend or co-worker, volunteer your name every time. Do this even when you have met the other person at another affair. It's not only a practical solution for people who have trouble getting names right or who forget them, but if they do remember your name, your doing this makes you look modest and makes the other person feel important. But after that, try something like:

> "Aren't you on the Board of Directors for this organization? I've admired your efforts for a long time. My name is Ron Coles. Do you know many of these people? I don't think I know anyone!"
>
> "Are there many people here tonight from your company?"
>
> "Do you know the organizers?"
>
> "Do you live in the area?"
>
> "Do you live nearby, or do you still have a bit of a commute left this evening?"
>
> "How are you involved with this group?"
>
> "How did you become interested in this organization?"
>
> "How were your holidays?"
>
> "I can't get over how many people turned out for this. Would you have expected it?"
>
> "I don't suppose you'd be able to recommend a good realtor?"
>
> "I see by your name tag that you're with Prime Consultants. I'm not familiar with them. Will you tell me a little about them?"
>
> "I've always wanted to ask someone why a band has to completely drown out all conversation."
>
> "I've recently joined this organization and I am very, very impressed with it."
>
> "Jenny! How's life treating you? Did you and your husband ever find an apartment?"
>
> "Someone did a great job of planning this event."
>
> "Someone pointed you out as one of the organizers, and I wanted to tell you what a superb job you've done."
>
> "This is one of the most worthwhile causes there is. How did you get interested in it?"
>
> "Would you point out the committee chair for me? I don't know her except by name."

"You're a wonderful dancer. Have you taken lessons? I'm thinking ballroom dancing lessons would be fun."

"Your face is familiar, but I don't think we've ever met. My name is Geraldine Montsford."

If They Say... You Say

Keep thinking of conversation as a tennis game. The idea is to keep the ball in play. If the ball is hit to you, return it to the other person in such a way that they will be able to hit it back. Your response should both link up with the last remark made by the other person and provide a bridge to their next remark. On the other hand, when a conversation is not enjoyable, do not return the ball (politely, of course), and the conversation will soon dry up.

If They Say	You Say
"Hi! I'm Gina Butler, with Freeman Bernina."	"I'm pleased to meet you. My name is Frances Burney and I believe you went to school with my brother."
"How do you know our hosts?"	"Our children attend the local school together. What about you?"
"I understand you're in Human Resources. Actually I'm looking for a job at the moment."	"Why don't you call the office tomorrow and make an appointment for an interview?"
"Who organizes these things? They invited way too many people."	"Really."
"No. I don't read."	"Oh. How about movies? Have you seen anything good lately?"
"I'm working to defeat the incumbent mayor. We've got to get rid of that crook. I wonder if you..."	"Excuse me, I can't talk politics on an empty stomach. I'm going to check out the buffet."
"Hi! I'm Soraya Saigh, and I can't think where our paths have crossed before."	"I've been wondering the same thing and have decided it was either at last year's banquet or at the midsummer conference."

"I wonder how much they paid for that chandelier."

"Congratulations on your Circle of Excellence Award tonight!"

"May I get you a fresh drink? I'm heading for the bar."

"Thanks! Aren't you good to remember one face among so many! What department are you in?"

Closing Lines

Because most people know they must mingle, you shouldn't have too much trouble ending one conversation so that you can wander to another group. But if you do, say something like:

"I'd like to have a word with the events coordinator this evening, but I certainly have enjoyed getting to know you."

"I hope we can do business together someday."

"I'll give you a call."

"I ought to go say hello to my boss. Nice meeting you!"

"I think I'll make a return trip to the buffet. Enjoy the rest of the evening."

"It looks as though the evening was great success—and it's in such a good cause. Good-night now."

"It's been great talking with you. We'll have to get together sometime."

"I've enjoyed meeting you—perhaps I'll see you later in the evening."

"I want to see if there are any other people from my company here."

"Let's not wait so long until our next visit."

"Say, do you know Kevin Wooster? Let me introduce you to him."

"Yes, good to talk with you, too."

(See Chapter 1 for more ways to end a conversation.)

CHAPTER 12

Talking With Anyone at Social Events

> *There are two kinds of people in this life:*
> *Those who walk into a room and say, "Well,*
> *here I am!" And those who walk in and say,*
> *"Ahh, there you are."*
>
> —Leil Lowndes

Introduction

All enjoyable social events—from elegant dinner parties to noisy family reunions to elegant-noisy cocktail parties—require some skill at small talk. If you're lucky, the opening exchanges will spark an in-depth conversation, the beginning of a cherished friendship, or a valued networking connection. With the right attitude, however, small talk can be satisfying, entertaining, and memorable even if it doesn't lead to anything more important.

Before You Arrive

The surest route to social disaster is to arrive at a gathering feeling that you are uninteresting. Beforehand, remind yourself that you were invited to this affair. Someone must appreciate you enough to want you there. Think over a few of your successes, the times you've enjoyed yourself at other gatherings.

Once you've persuaded yourself that you are appealing and personable and enjoy a certain rudimentary command of the language, forget yourself! Do not, absolutely not, think about yourself again until you are on your way home.

After you've cleared your head of yourself, turn your mind outward. Prepare to meet some intriguing people. You don't know yet how or why they are exciting, but you will—slowly—discover this. Think about the ones you know will be there. Imagine what you might like to ask them, or what you talked about the last time you saw them.

Always go into a situation expecting to be welcomed and accepted—nothing dramatic, certainly, but you anticipate warm smiles from those you'll meet. If you calmly expect this, you will get it. In turn, be prepared to be friendly and interested in others.

> *To talk easily with people, you must firmly believe that either you or they are interesting. And even then it's not easy.*
> —MIGNON McLAUGHLIN

A fairly recent phenomenon is the impact of the business world on the social world. People used to leave ample room in their lives for socializing—from gathering on front porches to keeping an unlocked door for family and friends to stopping for a chat at every store in town.

Today, the hurry-hurry world of the Internet, instant messaging, e-mail, and the cell phone has made us impatient with the slower pace of our personal relationships. We click on a link and bingo! we are taken directly to whatever we need. Seconds later, we know our order is in the mail. If we have to wait for something to download, we're indignant. Faster seems to equal better. We expect friends and family to react quickly to our questions, our concerns, and our needs. We want them to download a conversation as efficiently as our favorite website downloads an article.

We speak in acronyms (CIA, CEO, COD, CPA, CBS, CNN, CPR, CST—and that's only a few combinations from one letter of the alphabet), in abbreviations, or in shortened words ("Just a sec!").

This hurry syndrome affects most of us and is something to think about before arriving at a social gathering. Consciously put everything else out of your mind, slow yourself down, and prepare to roll with whatever comes. You can

> *Conversation was a kind of little flashlight, with which you explored caves you had never been in before. You never could guess, when you started, what you would find.*
> —MARGARET LEE RUNBECK

also stay hair-trigger tense if you like, but you won't be a people magnet.

In addition to preparing yourself to feel confident and relaxed, keep up to date on current events by reading at least one newspaper a day and possibly a weekly newsmagazine in addition to publications in your field. You don't have to know everything, but you should be prepared to discuss or at least look as though you know what they're talking about when someone brings up one of the headline issues of the day.

First Moves

One of the most common and effective ways to make contact with a new person or someone who looks slightly familiar is to extend your hand for a handshake while simultaneously giving your name. "Hi. Carlos Rodriguez." Most people will respond with their name. Then, of course, the ball is back in your court, so be prepared with a sentence or question to keep things going.

Exchanging names at the beginning is always a good idea. If you wait until you're knee-deep in a fascinating conversation, it's awkward to have to go back and introduce yourselves as if you had no history at all.

After you've used this technique a few times, you will feel comfortable during those first few seconds of any small talk.

Start talking about any trivial item and, by means of careful back-and-forthing, reach for a topic of interest to both of you. Trust the conversation to unfold. If you stay alert and return any balls your talking partner lobs to you, you will be as expert as anyone in the conversation business.

Your social event might not be taking place up in the hills, but be willing to go through a warm-up period. Edging into a conversation so as not to offend is an excellent way to begin.

> *Up here in the hills you hardly ever get down to business right off. First you say your howdys and then you talk about anything else but what you come for, and finally, when mosquitoes start to bite, you say what's on your mind. But you always edge into it, not to offend.*
> —Phyllis Reynolds Naylor

Do's

▶ Smile and make eye contact with your conversation partners.

▶ Focus on the other person. Forget about your appearance, your intelligence, your wit, or your social skills. Ignore the ceiling fan, the spilled drink on the other side of the room, the shriek of laughter behind you. If you give the other person your undiluted attention, you will automatically appear good-looking, smart, funny, and socially savvy.

Share something of yourself. Years ago, Edmond and Jules de Goncourt wrote, "Never speak of yourself to others; make them talk about themselves instead: therein lies the whole art of pleasing. Everyone knows it and everyone forgets it." Perhaps. Although the de Goncourt brothers have something of a point, it is flawed. If everyone refused to speak about themselves while simultaneously trying to make others do so, there would be no conversation at all. By all means, show interest in others. But there are conversational accounts to be balanced. If the other person tosses out a bit of personal information, you must ante up with something similar.

- ▶ Make your conversation a combination of statements ("I heard their daughter is a responsible babysitter"), questions ("Do you live in the neighborhood?"), and bits of self-revelation ("I met Justin in the service").

- ▶ Aim for a balance between telling something interesting about yourself (Henry Van Dyke said, "Modest egotism is the salt of conversation. You do not want too much of it; but if it is altogether omitted, everything tastes flat") and making yourself look a little too good (According to Mary H. Waldrip, "When someone sings his own praises, he always gets the tune too high").

- ▶ Include everyone in your small group in the talk. Watch for the more reserved person who's trying desperately to contribute something and say, "Paul? You were going to say something?" Or, to anyone who hasn't gotten the floor, "Jean, you were there, weren't you? What did you think?"

Strangers... are just your friends that you don't know yet.
—MARGARET LEE RUNBECK

In a group of six or fewer individuals, all should be included in the same topic. For two to branch off and talk quietly while the others are still on the topic makes people uneasy. Either slip away from the group if you are the twosome, or take part in the general discussion.

- ▶ Cultivate tact. Learn to watch people's faces and body language. A conversation is, by definition, the work of two or more people. The more you help others be part of it, the more successful your conversation will be, and the more well liked you will be.

- ▶ Avoid one-word answers. If you are asked a close-ended question where the only answers are "yes" or "no" ("Do you play golf?"), add something to your response ("No. But I watched the Open on television last week. Did you see it?") Otherwise the conversation will come to a standstill.

▶ Watch for clues that the other person is losing interest in you or the conversation. Often this is nothing personal. Most people at social gatherings have inner clocks that signal when it's time to move on.

In addition, because of the limits of social conversation, you will reach a point where you must either dive deeper into the topic or abandon it in the interests of mingling. The first choice is not a good one because others may get restive. A social event isn't the best occasion for a deep and meaningful discussion.

> *Small talk isn't supposed to be brilliant. Everyone is trite. Everyone engages in "small talk" that doesn't say anything clever or significant. This sort of small talk is necessary to get the wheels turning.*
> —LEE GIBLIN

Allow a little silence into your conversation. Silence can be warm, hostile, neutral, challenging, or passive-aggressive. But when it's a comfortable silence, it gives the less quick among us a chance to speak, and it relaxes everyone. If you yourself are a quieter sort of person, honor that. Let others know you are participating by means of some encouraging mutters or phrases and your interested attention. It is the obviously bored and supercilious nonspeaker who is a problem, not the genuinely reserved individual. In addition, there is always the possibility identified by Mary Lowry.

> *There are very few people who don't become more interesting when they stop talking.*
> —MARY LOWRY

▶ Ask good questions to keep the conversation going (see Chapter 5).

Don'ts

▶ Don't monopolize the conversation. You are talking *with* someone, not *to* someone. If you aren't sure whether you are monopolizing the conversation, keep track of approximately how many minutes you speak compared to how many minutes the others speak. If your small group seems genuinely interested in what you are saying (usually indicated by asking good questions), you may have found kindred spirits. But if the others' participation consists of one-word interjections or silence, this is usually only politeness and you have probably been monopolizing the conversation.

- Don't say too much. People you've just met do not appreciate hearing about your divorce (no matter how sympathetic they seem), your complaints about the IRS, a situation that makes you extremely angry, the ups and downs of your love life, how much money you make (or spend), or the particular addiction you are currently dealing with. Small talk is a buffer zone where the white flag can fly and those under its protection can enjoy conversations without watching for land mines. Sensitive, emotional, or very private information should wait until a deeper relationship has been established.

> *One never repents of having spoken too little, but often of having spoken too much.*
> —PHILIPPE DE COMMYNES

- Don't speak too loudly. Obviously, most people who do this are unaware of it, so you might be an unknowing offender in this respect. The next time you are conversing in a group, take a moment to contrast your decibels with others'.

- Don't interrupt people or finish their sentences. In polite company, whoever is speaking has the floor; others wait a beat or two before putting in their two cents' worth to make sure the other person has finished speaking.

- Don't look at your watch or around the room while someone is speaking with you (use your trip to the refreshment table to see who else is there). As Anne-Sophie Swetchine said several centuries ago, "Attention is a silent and perpetual flattery." So pay attention. The other person will go home thinking you are a gifted conversationalist.

- Don't correct anyone's pronunciation, grammar, or facts, unless, as in the case of facts, it is important to tactfully make the correction. There are actually people who pride themselves on setting others straight. If someone does this to you, say "Thank you," and continue with what you were saying.

- Don't even think about asking—no matter how indirectly, cleverly, or subtly—for advice from a plumber, computer technician (very popular these days), stockbroker, landscaper, or other professional.

> *The person talking to you never looks directly you, but rather around the room, searching for the answer to the universal cocktail party question, "Who's here tonight?"*
> —LETITIA BALDRIGE

- Don't use jargon, insider language, slang, or off-color language at social events unless you are sure you are with like-minded individuals... or unless the other person starts it first.
- Don't try to outdo others. If they've been to Paris for a week, don't tell about the time you went for a month. You can certainly discuss what you both loved about Paris, but be careful about stealing anyone's pleasure. Even you—later—won't like yourself for it.
- Think twice before telling a joke. (See Chapter 6.)
- Don't assume the other person is married because you are or is single because you are or is heterosexual because you are. Instead of asking, "Are you married?" or "Do you have children?" say, "Tell me about your family" or "Do you have family in the area?"
- Don't discuss your children in detail, except with friends who know them and truly want to hear about them. When other people ask how your children are, it is much like the ritual "How do you do?" They want you to say, "Fine," and talk about something of more interest to them.

> *Parents of young children should realize that few people, and maybe no one, will find their children as enchanting as they do.*
> —BARBARA WALTERS

Special Situations

- If you commit a faux pas—and why shouldn't you? Everyone else does—do not panic. Saying something you regret, spilling a drink, or calling someone by the wrong name are all fairly commonplace occurrences. Although some people handle this ironically or humorously ("I'm known far and wide for my lack of good taste" "Did I really say that?"), the most universally acceptable remedy is a heartfelt apology ("I'm truly sorry. I'll call you tomorrow to find out how I can replace it") followed by never referring to it again. (See Chapter 7 for more help on faux pas.)
- Should you encounter celebrities at an event, it's best if someone introduces you to them, but you can tactfully introduce yourself if it doesn't mean elbowing your way

> *Tact is the art of making people feel at home when that's where you wish they were.*
> —ANN LANDERS

through a crowd to get to them. A few guidelines: (1) Don't gush, piling superlative upon superlative—it's unlikely that what you're saying is new to them; a brief one-sentence acknowledgment of their accomplishments is sufficient ("I admire your work very much"). (2) Be brief, and move along so others can have a minute with them. If you have a reason for wanting to speak with the person, a public gathering is not the place. Ask someone in the celebrity's retinue about the best way to get in touch with the person or their staff. (3) Do not express astonishment that the person is younger, older, fatter, shorter, balder than you thought. (4) Do not approach anyone who is eating or trying to relax. (5) Do not use their first name unless you are invited to; no matter how familiar the person seems to you, you are a stranger to them. (6) Should you feel compelled to ask for an autograph, secure pen and paper first. (7) Don't rush to apologize for not having seen the person's last movie or read the person's last book.

Should you find yourself chatting with a celebrity by yourself, steer clear of the fan questions that they have answered so many times ("What did it feel like to...?" or, worse, "Have you ever met Josh Hartnett/Madonna?"). Ask something neutral: "Have you had a chance to see much of our town?" "You know it's tornado season here. Have you ever seen one?"

Celebrities usually know about more than just their profession so you might explore topics like sports, travel, gardening, new books, stamp collecting, animals, or cooking.

Some people have been known to approach a familiar-looking person at a party and ask, "Do I know you? Are you somebody? Are you anyone important?" Really.

Topics of Conversation

Social gatherings produce some far-ranging conversational topics, and any list of suggested conversational topics is bound to be arbitrary. A topic that is acceptable and even desirable in one group might be unacceptable and perhaps disastrous in a group standing a few feet away. The key is knowing your audience. When you're with family and friends or with people with whom you've worked for years, you might be able to bring up almost any subject you like.

However, when you are with people you don't know intimately, in a business or social setting where small talk is the order of the day, you might want to familiarize yourself with the lists below of what to talk about and what not to talk about. Essentially, this will give you "conversation lite."

The most important caveat is to avoid controversial topics. Aim for lightweight subjects of general interest and of no possible offense to anyone.

You must depend on your own good sense of what is appropriate. The topic of money used to be verboten at social affairs, for example, but on many occasions today, it is simply another interesting topic.

Topics to Consider

Anecdotes, opinions, observations

Books

Climate changes

Community events, issues

Computers

Family—theirs and yours

Favorite cartoon strip

Food being served

Hobbies

Local events

Movies

New gadgets

New restaurants in town

Noncontroversial newspaper articles

Pets

Real estate

Sports

Television shows

The arts

Traffic

Vacation plans

Weather

Today money is a favorite topic of conversation in many settings. The financial page of the daily newspaper is read about as avidly as the sports page or the comics. There has probably never been a cocktail party at which the subject of taxes, the cost of living, or the price of real estate has not been discussed. In gossip circles, who did what with whom is rivaled only by who paid how much for what.
—HERB GOLDBERG AND ROBERT T. LEWIS

Topics to Avoid

- A party to which others weren't invited
- Blatant networking
- Comments on other people's attire, behavior, speech
- Complaints
- Confidential issues
- Controversial issues (e.g., abortion, assisted suicide, capital punishment, welfare system, affirmative action, prayer and sex education in the schools, PETA, the environment)
- Criticisms
- Death
- Detailed accounts of your prowess at golf or other sports
- Domestic revelations
- Excessive shop talk
- Gossip
- Lengthy description of your travels
- Money
- Personal failures, flaws, and foibles
- Personal problems
- Politics
- Prices of things
- Put-downs
- Recap of a TV show you saw
- Religion
- Salaries—yours or other people's
- Sex
- The other person's love life
- Work problems
- Your children—how brilliant they are
- Your divorce
- Your grandchildren
- Your health, illnesses

> *Don't indulge in gossip...People who throw mud always manage to end up getting a little on themselves.*
> —ANN LANDERS

Conversation Starters

The classic way to begin a conversation is to make a low-key statement about the occasion or the surroundings, and then to ask an open-ended question: "I understand Robert and Julia did that astonishing rose garden themselves. How do you know them?"

The first time it's up to you to speak, try something like:

"Ann Freeman [shaking hands]. We met at last year's picnic."

"Are you a Mac person or a PC person?"

"Are you by any chance a Lakers fan?"

"Are you much of a film-goer? I'm a movie buff myself, and I'm always looking for other aficionados."

"Are you new to the neighborhood? Are you settling in? If I can help with anything, let me know."

"Are you reading anything good these days?"

"Did we set a record-high temperature today?"

"Did you have a good weekend?"

"Did you know that woman over there is our new mayor? She's not only charming, but she seems very capable."

"Did you notice the rock wall in the back yard?"

"Did you run into that closed stretch of the freeway getting here tonight?"

"Do you garden? I was trying to think how to keep the rabbits out, and it occurred to me to see if you had any ideas."

"Do you know everyone here?"

"Do you know many of the guests?"

"Do you know what time it is?"

"Do you live around here?"

"Everyone seems to be enjoying the party."

"Excuse me, but do you know the fellow there in the green tie? I think I've met him somewhere, but I can't remember where."

Ideal conversation must be an exchange of thought, and not, as many of those who worry most about shortcomings believe, an eloquent exhibition wit or oratory.

—EMILY POST

"Have you been out on the balcony? The view is stupendous."

"Have you lived here long?"

"Have you spoken to the woman in the red suit? She knows everything about palmistry."

"Have you tried the sushi?"

"Hello! I'm Barbara Bowles, Betsy's sister from Boston."

"Hi! I'm Walford Springs, and you are...?"

"How do you know our hosts?"

"How's life been treating you lately?"

"I can't get over the magical effect so many candles have on this room."

"I don't suppose you know the name of this song."

"I don't suppose you've seen the new Craig Hurley movie?"

"If you're who I think you are, I've heard the most wonderful things about you!"

"I hear you're the new chair of the Cinco de Mayo festival—congratulations!"

"I just finished the best book—if you have the time, you might want to take a look at it."

"I'm not familiar with your company. Will you give me a little background?"

"I'm really looking forward to this weekend—what about you?"

"I'm wilting from the heat. What would your ideal climate be?"

"I noticed your logo from the tennis club. Could you recommend someone to give me lessons?"

"I once spilled a glass of wine on a new beige carpet and, ever since, I've been afraid to eat or drink anything at one of these mingling affairs."

"I understand you're an astronomer. Does your interest in stars go all the way back to your childhood, or is it more recent?"

"I've seen you around the neighborhood, but I don't think we've met. My name is Julia Romero."

"I wonder who catered this. The hors d'oeuvres are as unusual as they are delicious."

"I worked right through lunch today, so excuse me if I dig in."

"My wife and I just moved into the neighborhood. We're three houses down from you. Would you know any good babysitters?"

"Say, have you had deer in your yard this fall?"

"Seeing the kids playing in the park on the way here reminded me of summers when I was a kid. What did you do during vacation when you were growing up?"

"Someone told me that all the vegetables we're eating came from our host's garden."

"Someone told me that I should come and talk with you."

"So what was your day like today?"

"The buffet is to die for—perhaps because I am hopeless in the kitchen. How about you? Do you cook?"

> *The success of conversation consists less in being witty than in bringing out wit in others; the man who leaves after talking with you, pleased with himself and his own wit, is perfectly pleased with you.*
>
> —LA BRUYÈRE

"This music reminds me of when I was sixteen, and music was everything to me. Were you like that?"

"This music takes me right back to our senior prom. Where does it take you?"

"We're new in the area. How cold can it get here anyway?"

"What a buffet! I see you found the shrimp, too."

"What brings you to this part of the country?"

"What brought you to this area?"

"What do you think about the bookshelves Dave built?"

"Where do you call home?"

"Will you go anywhere special this summer?"

"You look familiar, but I'm not sure we've ever met."

"You look so fit. May I ask what sort of a fitness regimen you follow?"

"You're in retail, I understand. How, in general, has the Internet affected your business?"

"Yum, these are the best spring rolls!"

If They Say...You Say

Note the pattern below: an appropriate response is followed by a question so that you keep the conversational ball in the air.

If They Say	You Say
"Hi! I'm John Corcoran."	"Glad to meet you. I'm Tonya Hughes, a friend and co-worker of Jenny's. How do you know Jenny and Vince?"
"Um, do I know you?"	[Smiling] "Well, only you would know for sure. I'm Jessica Alba, and I live down the street. Do you live in this area?"
"I'm really embarrassed, but I've forgotten your name."	"Please don't think anything of it. I've forgotten my share of names. It's Leroy Asche. I think we met at their holiday party last year. Weren't you there?"
"We just moved into the neighborhood last week."	"Welcome! You're going to love it. I'd be happy to tell you anything I can about the area and share names of sitters and piano teachers. Do you need anything like that?"
"Have you tried the homemade parfait?"	"I have. And I asked for the recipe. Do you like to cook?"
"Have you seen the collection of children's tea sets?"	"No! Where is it? Will you show me? Is this an interest of yours?"
"Do you live in the neighborhood?"	"No, I live in the Nash Village area. How about you?"
"Do you know when the quartet is going to play?"	"Around eight o'clock. Are you interested in music?"
"I don't know a soul here. Do you?"	"Actually, I know two people. Come with me and I'll introduce you. How do you come to be here if you don't know anyone?"

Closing Lines

When it's time to move on to another group, you can bring your conversation to a close by saying something like:

[A firm handshake and] "It's been great talking with you."

"Excuse me, I need to use the restroom."

"I can still hear my mother saying, 'Mingle! Mingle!' I should probably ...well, you know, mingle!"

"I'd like to have lunch. Here's my card if you want to give me a call when you're free."

"I have to go say a word to Frank, but I hope our paths cross again sometime."

"I hope you enjoy the rest of the evening."

"I'll send you a copy of that article we talked about."

"I'm going to get something to drink. Perhaps I'll see you later."

"I'm going to start saying my good-byes, but I've very much enjoyed our conversation."

"I'm looking forward to seeing you again sometime."

"I need to circulate—there are so many people I don't know here tonight."

"I promised Karen I'd help refill the trays. I'd better go check."

"I see Chris Dodge. Why don't you join me and I'll introduce you."

"I think I'm going to head for the buffet table before all the crab cakes are gone."

"It's been great getting to know you."

"I've really enjoyed our conversation. Maybe I'll see you later in the evening."

"I want to speak with Lee before she leaves."

"I won't monopolize you any further, but it's been good talking with you."

"Maria's been signaling me—I'd better see what she wants."

"Thanks for introducing me to the world of inkwell collecting."

CHAPTER 13

Talking With Anyone in Public Places

Each person's life is lived as a series of conversations.

—Deborah Tannen

Introduction

Conversation in public places has decreased dramatically in the last century. Primarily because of the car and the television, people no longer stand chatting on sidewalks or in front of stores in small downtowns. Because of the hurry-hurry influence of contemporary business life and the instant responses of the computer, we are impatient when we must stand in line. Striking up a conversation with someone might slow us down. What if it's our turn to check out and the other person still wants to talk?

However, there are times when you will find yourself exchanging a few words with someone in the uncontrolled spaces between home and work: airports, airplanes, supermarkets, bookstores, laundromats, malls, waiting rooms, bars, concert and movie lines, dog parks, resort pools, post offices.

You run into two kinds of people in public: those you know and those you don't know. Of those you know, some might be social acquaintances, others might be business connections.

Social acquaintances are easiest because you have a history, you know what to talk about, and you can have a more personal conversation. With people from work, you are warmer than you are with strangers, but you do not suddenly become friends simply because you've run into each other outside

Remember that the people you are talking to are a hundred times more interested in themselves and their wants and problems than they are in you and your problems.

—Dale Carnegie

work. A certain dignity and a bit of formality are involved. With strangers you are courteous, you show by a smile and nod that you mean them well, and if you talk it is of generalities and commonplaces.

These happenstance meetings are usually too short for any meaningful exchanges. Instead, the most inane conversations are acceptable and, in fact, appropriate. It is understood that saying something bland is a way of acknowledging that the other person is a human being without, however, invading the person's privacy or wanting to become best friends in the next few minutes.

Most often, a simple exchange is the norm: "I wish I'd gotten a cart. I only meant to pick up a couple of items." "I do the same thing." A commiserating sigh or a shake of the head and you're finished.

At other times, when you find yourself in someone's company for more than a few minutes, the conversation might be extended. But both people must make sure the other person is interested in talking. One person wanting to talk and one person not wanting to talk do not a conversation make. When one statement is met with another and a question, and that is met with a statement and a question, it's likely that a casual conversation is underway.

In public, people have a curious there and not-there status, which is why you acknowledge those around you but do not enter into a full-fledged relationship with them.

Because of changing cultural priorities—primarily the isolation brought about by long workdays, too many hours alone in a car commuting to work, and hours in front of the television—most of us are experiencing a sense of isolation. Many of us look upon others as threats to our privacy, resources, and success. For these reasons, our contacts with each other in public need to be as kind, supportive, and engaging as we can make them, not only as a sign of our goodwill but for our long-term well-being.

Do's

▶ Acknowledge others with a smile and a nod, when appropriate. Respond to a greeting at the same level it was offered: "Nice day." "Sure is." Obviously, exchanges vary in degree depending on whether the other person is unknown to you, a co-worker, or a good friend. It is still always a good practice to match your level of warmth, expression of interest, or length of conversation to the other person's. Being "in sync" produces comfort and mutual liking.

> *What are compliments? They are things you say to people when you don't know what else to say.*
> —CONSTANCE JONES

- Say something complimentary as long as it isn't too personal: "What a darling child!" "I couldn't help admiring your umbrella." "May I say that you were wonderfully patient with the receptionist?" "Your tattoo is magnificent!" "I agree with the message on your T-shirt." "That's my favorite breed of dog."
- Take advantage of visual clues on which to base a conversation: Is the person's cart full of gardening equipment? Do they have a dog on a leash? Are they wearing the same running shoes you buy? Is their political button consonant with your preferences? Are they accompanied by children? Is their luggage covered with stickers from all over the world? Are they wearing a sweatshirt from your alma mater?
- Allow others their personal space. When in public it is important to appear nonthreatening and respectful. If you see someone doing or wearing or reading something unusual, do not ask for explanations.
- Include those who use wheelchairs in your glance. Too many people will smile at a room full of strangers who are more or less at eye level and forget about those who are not. No special treatment is necessary. Just involve everyone nearby if you greet people or ask a question or start a conversation.
- If you are standing near someone using a white cane, it is courteous to say hello and perhaps add a comment about the cold or the humidity or the environment. They will know you are near, so it isn't as though you will startle them. A simple question ("Have you been here before?" "Have you ever heard this speaker?" "Is this your first time in Phoenix?") will let you know if the other person is interested in conversing.

> *Should you happen to notice that another person is extremely tall or overweight, eats too much or declines convivial drinks, has red hair or goes about in a wheelchair, ought to get married or ought not to be pregnant—see if you can refrain from bringing these astonishing observations to that person's attention.*
>
> —JUDITH MARTIN

Don'ts

- In the case of strangers, you don't need to begin by exchanging names and shaking hands, although sometimes after a good conversation, you might want to do so in order to further your acquaintance.

- Never pursue a conversation if the other person is not responding. No matter how bored you are standing in line or sitting in the waiting room, other people are not obliged to provide you with entertainment. This might seem obvious, but some people have such a violent need to talk, or are so determined to win over the other person, that they seem impervious to hints that the other person wants to be left alone.

> *They...talk simply because they think sound is more manageable than silence.*
> —Margaret Halsey

- Do not insist on conversing with your seatmate on an airplane, train, bus, or subway. If you know yourself as someone who enjoys chatting with strangers, make arrangements for other ways to pass the time, because your chances of finding someone who also likes to chat with strangers are slim. The approved behavior is to nod and smile politely in their direction as you settle yourself.

   Should you come upon a seatmate who repeatedly tries to engage you in conversation, say something like:

   "Excuse me, but I need to sleep on this flight."

   "I can't hear a thing on these planes, so I don't enjoy trying to converse."

   "I'm sorry but I've been looking forward to this flight all day so that I could be quiet and relax."

   "I never talk when I'm flying—it makes me nervous."

   "I really need this time to myself."

   "I seem to be coming down with a cold, and it hurts to talk. Unfortunately, I can't hear much either."

   "I think I'm coming down with something—I really shouldn't breathe in your direction."

   "My throat is terribly sore and I need to rest it. I hope it's not strep."

   "Say, does your family have enough life insurance? I have a whole range of policies that cover practically any situation."

- Don't touch someone you don't know. No matter how friendly the tap on the arm or the hand on the shoulder, it is most often taken as intrusive, threatening, or unwelcome.

- Don't ask questions that are too personal. This is always a judgment call, but in general the following questions would be considered inappropriate:

"Are you married?"

"Are you someone important?"

"Are you sure you'll be able to open that window in case of an emergency?"

"Do you dye your hair?"

"Do you ever give away free samples?"

"Do you have children?"

"Do you live in a house or in an apartment?"

"Do you realize how harmful it is to smoke?"

"Have you ever thought of getting into an exercise program?"

"How old are you?"

"I've always wanted to ask someone why they read romance novels. Can you tell me?"

"What did you pay for your ticket?"

"Where did you graduate from college?"

"Why are you wearing cowboy boots?"

Special Situations

▶ If someone is wearing a button or shirt with a message, or has a tattoo in a visible place, it is usually accepted—and sometimes welcome—to mention them.

▶ You might be caught off-guard when you're running late and you encounter someone who wants to chat. Say something like:

"Excuse me for interrupting, but I simply must keep on schedule today. Give me a call, will you?"

"How frustrating! I've been wanting to see you, but right now I can't stop for even a second. May I call you tonight?"

Talking's just a nervous habit.
—MARTHA GRIMES

"I'm five minutes late already, or I'd love to chat. Can I take a rain-check on a good visit?"

"Just my luck, to run into you when I haven't a minute to spare."

"What a pity. I'm late for an appointment. Call me tomorrow and we'll catch up with each other."

- If the sight of a celebrity causes you to become another person—one with virtually no dignity or self-control—and you absolutely need to speak with the person and possibly obtain an autograph, at least remember a few things: (1) Don't approach them while they're eating or trying to climb into a cab or are in the middle of something they appear to need to do. (2) Wait your turn to approach them. (3) Be very, very brief and do not gush—a simple expression of appreciation is enough. (4) Have a pen and piece of paper ready for their autograph. (5) Move on.

- If you are asked for spare change, your response will depend on your beliefs: you feel no one should "encourage" the homeless or you believe they will only spend it on drink or drugs so, as a matter of principle, you never give any money to them; every morning you put a certain amount of money in your pocket and give it to the first such person you encounter; you plan your charitable giving at your desk and feel it is better to give to an organization that can monitor the uses of your money. However, whatever your decision, do not look past or through street people. Say "Good morning" or smile and nod.

> *Never, never ask an author what he is going to write next, a painter what subject he is going to depict next. They much prefer talking about their past achievements.*
> —LILLIAN EICHLER

Topics of Conversation

Almost any topic can be good or bad, depending on the context. Not all the suggestions below will be correct in all cases, but they might give you ideas. They are generally topics to open conversations with. If you and the other person find you enjoy talking, you can go to the next level and converse more personally and intensely, discussing work and families and experiences.

Topics to Consider

Anecdotes, opinions, observations

Book the other person is carrying: is it good? would you recommend it?

Dogs: what's your dog's name? what breed is it?

Do you know if this flight is overbooked?

Event you are about to see: what you've heard about it, how difficult it was to get tickets, what brought you here

Flying today: how stuffy it is in the cabins, how small the seats are, how seldom you get anything but a bag of pretzels

Hobbies: do you collect those? you must be a model-plane enthusiast

Local-interest issues: new civic center, library, public swimming pool, arts center, finally repairing potholes

Noncontroversial newspaper story of importance: earthquake, volcano erupting, 102-car traffic pileup

Sports

Surroundings: comments about the room, building, area, auditorium

Traffic or parking problems in the area

Weather: unusual, threatening, effect on event or future plans

Where to find: a good restaurant, nearest Starbucks, a store that sells used books.

> *Good-nature is more agreeable in conversation than wit, and gives a certain air to the countenance which is more amiable than beauty.*
> —JOSEPH ADDISON

Topics to Avoid

Complaining about delays, inconveniences, mix-ups

Controversial issues

Criticisms of the surroundings, the event, the food

Flying today—how scary it is

Illnesses

Money: how much things cost, salaries—yours or theirs

Off-color jokes

Personal questions about the other person

Politics

Religion

Remarks about people nearby

Sex

Your health

Your personal problems

> *Don't talk about diseases, hospitals, ailments, operations. Above all, don't talk about your own symptoms.*
> —LILLIAN EICHLER

Conversation Starters

People You Don't Know

"Any predictions on tonight's game?"

"Are you a member?"

"Do I know you from somewhere?"

"Do you come here often?"

"Do you know anything about this speaker?"

"Do you know where I could find a clock-repair shop?"

"Do you live around here?"

"Do you shop here often?"

"Excuse me, do you know where the nearest florist is?"

"Have you always lived here?"

"Have you heard any good things about this movie?"

"I can't believe how smoky it is in here—I didn't think you could smoke in places like this anymore."

"I don't suppose you saw 'Survivor' last night. I missed it and don't know who was kicked off."

"I ended up parking on the street—do you know if there's a parking ramp around here?"

"I see you at work, but I don't think we've met. My name is ..."

"I see you play tennis. Could you recommend a tennis club?"

"I see you're a PC computer person. I'm a Mac person myself. What do you see as the advantages of a PC over a Mac?"

"Is New Orleans your final destination, or are you making a connection there?"

"This is my first time at this bank—have you been banking here long?"

"This is my first trip to Lisbon. Have you been there before?"

Every social encounter is rich with blunders, inanities, and foolishness. Very little of what is said is really apt, still less important, still less eloquent. But people accept, respond to, echo, laugh with, and generally appreciate the stumbling attempts others make at conversation because they appreciate the show of interest, the willingness to take part.

—DEBORAH TANNEN

"This is the same Muzak my foot doctor plays—and my feet are getting nervous."

"What do you think about airport security these days?"

"What do you think about the automated checkout machines?"

People You Know

"Do you have plans for the holidays? Going away? Staying home? Having visitors?"

"Frank! How's life treating you?"

"Have you been a patient of hers for long?"

"Hello! I ran into Jennifer the other day, and we talked about the three of us getting together for lunch."

"How did you find out about this auction?"

"I haven't seen you all summer. Have you been away?"

"Isn't this the greatest museum? They have the best Egyptian collection I've ever seen."

"I've always wanted to ask you where you find such delightful gifts, and now I know! This is a fabulous store."

"I've been thinking about you. What a coincidence!"

"Jean, nice to see you. How're Ed and the family?"

Never let an opportunity pass to give a well-deserved compliment.
—Ann Landers

"Just the person I wanted to see! Tell me how Justin is doing."

"Well, hello. I haven't seen you in a while."

"Weren't you about to move the last time I saw you?"

"What a surprise!"

"What brought you here today?"

"What prompted you to attend this concert?"

"What's your connection to this group?"

"William! How's it going?"

If They Say... You Say

If They Say	You Say
"Excuse me, may I get ahead of you in line? I'm in a hurry."	"Of course!"
"Excuse me, may I get ahead of you line? I'm in a hurry."	"Any other time it would in be fine. But I'm running late myself. Sorry."
"That's a beautiful ring. How much did you pay for it?"	"I don't remember."
"You know what I hate? People who wait until all their groceries are bagged and in the cart before they start writing their check."	"Really."
"That's one of the most handsome Golden Retrievers I've ever seen."	"Aren't you nice! And she's as well-behaved as she is good-looking. How do you know Golden Retrievers?"

Closing Lines

"Enjoy the show!"

"Good luck with your gardening."

"Good to see you again, Annette!"

"Have a wonderful time in Caracas."

"I enjoyed meeting you."

"It's been nice talking with you."

"I've enjoyed our conversation."

"Maybe our paths will cross again sometime"

"Say hello to Flo and the family for me, will you?"

"Take it easy!"

"There, that wasn't such a bad wait, thanks to you!"

"What a pleasure running into you."

CHAPTER 14

Talking With Anyone on the Telephone

*Hi, this is Sylvia. I'm not at home right
now, so when you hear the beep...hang up.*

—NICOLE HOLLANDER

Introduction

Assuming you reach an actual person when you call, remember that there are two kinds of people in this world: those who like the telephone and perk up when it rings, and those whose nervous system goes into fight-or-flight mode and exclaim, in the words of Dorothy Parker, "What fresh hell is this?"

Knowing that you might have reached someone who's growling under their breath, be prepared to be brief and direct. If the other person gives signs of wanting to prolong the conversation—and you have the time for it—you can relax and enjoy it. Otherwise, friendly and succinct is what you want to be.

> *Oh, how often I wished that Thomas A. Watson had laid a restraining hand on A.G. Bell's arm and said to him, "Let's not and say we did."*
>
> —JEAN MERCIER

There are three types of phone calls: (1) business calls, (2) personal calls, and (3) consumer calls.

Business calls are generally made from the workplace. They have a specific purpose (imagine calling the line boss to chat) and are usually brief. If the issue needs more discussion, you will probably arrange a meeting, unless you are on other sides of the continent.

You begin with an inquiry about how things are going ("How is life treating you these days?"), but both of you know this is simply a formality to signal friendliness. The standard, "How's it going?" is met with, "Great. And you?" followed by "Couldn't be better. Listen, about the report you faxed me..."). You close with a friendly remark ("Take care.").

Personal calls are, well, personal, so you will manage those as you always have. (See Chapter 16 for a few general guidelines on talking with family and friends, and Chapter 17 for help with talking with someone in whom you're romantically interested.)

Consumer calls (making a doctor appointment, ordering merchandise, canceling a newspaper, calling in a prescription refill, checking on the availability of tires for your car) theoretically shouldn't be made from the workplace, but given that these calls must often take place between 9:00 and 5:00 you will be making them from work. It is thus even more important to be brief and businesslike. You will probably omit the friendly remarks fore and aft, saying instead, "I'm calling to renew a prescription." No need to make jolly. On the other hand, politeness and patience are essential.

Do's

▶ Your answering machine is often the first voice people encounter when trying to reach you. Please make your message brief. Everyone knows about beeps now and about leaving their name and number and most answering machines record the time of the call. A message can include your name or your number, a promise to return the call (although this too is understood today), and, if you like, some expression of pleasure at receiving the call.

"Fran Ryan here. Thanks for calling. Leave a message."

"Hi, this is Mary. Please leave a message."

"Hi! You've reached the Simpsons. We'll get back to you pronto because we're looking forward to talking with you."

"You've reached Patty Roebuck. I'm sorry I missed your call. Leave your name and number and I'll get back to you."

It is not rude to turn off your telephone by switching it on to an answering machine, which is cheaper and less disruptive than ripping it out of the wall. Those who are offended because they cannot always get through when they seek, at their own convenience, to barge in on people are suffering from a rude expectation.

—JUDITH MARTIN

> "You've reached Rory Field at Systems-a-Go-Go. I'll return your call as soon as I can."
>
> "You've reached 818-555-1234. Please leave a message and we'll return your call as soon as possible."

If your business calls are handled by an automated system, your callers should be greeted by a brief message and by not too many menu choices—if you can do anything about that.

Consider recording a fresh message every day. In a business situation, this gives you the appearance of being at your desk, expecting calls, and being prepared to deal with them. It is particularly helpful if you mention times you'll be away from your desk:

> "Thanks for calling. This is Ruby Bocuse on February 7. I will be at or near my desk all week, so you can expect a return call very soon."
>
> "You've reached Jerry Hardesty at Minkus Inc. It's Tuesday, September 14, and I'll be out of the office until the 16th. Leave a message and I'll call when I return."
>
> "You've reached Mary Kay Sanders at Pathways. If you're getting this message I am on another phone call. But I will be in the office all day today except for a meeting from 3:00 to 4:00 and will return your call as soon as I can."

▶ Let your answering machine take the call when you are with another person or too busy to talk. Answering the phone only to bark that you're busy and you'll call back is not any better than the answering machine.

▶ When you call someone, say who you are and make sure they are free to speak with you. In the best of all possible worlds, people would not answer a ringing phone unless they were free to take the call, but most people today are multitasking, so it's best to ask at the beginning if they have time for your call. And once you ask, "Is this a good time to speak with you?" be sure to wait for the response. Some people ask the question and then immediately start talking.

> *A ringing telephone is the insistent summons of modern life, and the decision not to take a call requires fortitude.*
> —STEPHANIE WINSTON

▶ When leaving a message on an answering machine, tell who you are in the beginning and then repeat it at the end of the call, spelling out your last name if it is not easily decoded. Give your telephone number slowly and clearly. It is helpful to then repeat it so that a person can double-check what they've jotted down without having to replay the call. Too many people speak quite nicely until they arrive at their telephone number, at which point they either sprint through it or mumble it unintelligibly because it is so familiar to them.

▶ Unless you are calling a friend for a catch-up chat, be brief. Very, very brief.

▶ When the callee's spouse, partner, or assistant answers the phone, say a sentence or two that recognizes they aren't part of the phone equipment:

"Good afternoon to you, too, Frida. This is Mac. How's it going? Is the boss available for a quick call?"

"Good morning, Ms. MacIntosh, this is Fred Marchant. And how are you today? Syl always speaks so highly of you. May I speak to him?"

"Hi Joan, This is Sybil. Before you connect me to Sam, how was your vacation?"

"Yes, this is Irene Nash calling for Penny Sears, but may I first say that you have the best telephone voice I've heard in years."

If you make a mistake and answer the phone only to find someone who has far too much time on their hands and an endless fund of anecdotes, commentaries, remarks, jokes, and random observations, say something like:

"I'd love to talk with you, but it's impossible just now. May I call you tomorrow?"

"I'm as busy as a moth in a muff at the moment. Let me call you later."

"I'm terribly sorry, but I simply must hang up. Either the house or my hair is on fire."

"I'm unbelievably busy this morning. Let me call you tonight."

"It's one of those days here—I really can't talk."

"Listen, all heck just broke loose around here. Can I call you back as soon as it settles?"

"They're cracking down on personal phone calls, Jack. We're going to have to talk another time."

▶ When telephoning family and friends, treat them as courteously as you would your business acquaintances: ask if they are free to talk, let them do half the talking, and be sensitive to cues that they are ready to bring the call to a close. Every few months you might think back over your personal calls to see if you were as polite and charming and thoughtful to your friends and family as you were to people in your work life.

In addition, although there are times when the phone call comes first, don't leave family and friends with the impression that anything that comes in on your cell phone has priority over them.

- Following a business call, acknowledge in writing what has been discussed: "Per our call this morning…" "As we decided on the telephone this afternoon…" "We'll go ahead with the work beginning…" "I'm glad you could reschedule our interview to…" This is insurance against forgetfulness and misunderstandings.

- Before putting someone on hold, ask if they would prefer that you or they call back. Some people don't mind being put on hold; others will hold it against you.

- When calling friends and family, check yourself every few minutes to make certain you are leaving the other person space in which to say something. The telephone has a curious effect on some people who, once started and not being able to see the other person, don't seem able to stop talking, linking one topic with the next so seamlessly that the other person can't get a word in edgewise. Ideally, each person gets to talk half the time.

> *At the end of every year, I add up the time that I have spent on hold and subtract it from my age. I don't count that time as really living. I spend more and more time on hold each year. By the time I die, I'm going to be quite young.*
>
> —RITA RUDNER

- When your caller does not give a name, but says abruptly, "May I talk to Florence?" you are welcome to say, "May I ask who's calling?" If you're answering for another person, you probably do not ask, "What do you want her for?" but you would say, "May I tell her who's calling?" Not identifying oneself is so thoughtless that you can defend yourself in any polite way you like.

Don'ts

- Don't let the telephone take over your life. If you don't have an assistant, get an answering machine. Return calls only at certain times of the day so that the whole day does not consist of telephone calls with a little work sandwiched between. Callers with a sense of entitlement are not going to make your life any easier whether you take their call now or return it later. The use of an answering machine tends to cut the total number of calls. In addition, people respect those who are a little hard to get. But these are by-products. Your aim is to accomplish something today. Make the phone work for you. Don't end up working for it.

▶ Don't call someone and say "Guess who." Even—perhaps especially—if you think they will identify you on the first guess and then shriek with delight, don't do it. Few people like it.

▶ Don't call anyone who's hospitalized or seriously ill at home unless you have been assured that they are able to take a call. Oddly enough, people with long-term illnesses that keep them at home would welcome more calls than they receive. However, the acutely ill will gladly trade your telephoned cheer and good wishes for some extra sleep and a pain pill.

> *The very instrument that was supposed to be the greatest time-saver in our history has turned into the biggest time-waster. The telephone causes more interruption and generates more stress than anything else in our business environment.*
> —CONNIE GLASER AND BARBARA STEINBERG SMALLEY

▶ Don't put anyone on the speakerphone without asking if that's agreeable. It's unnerving when you think you're speaking to one person to find that, in fact, there are five people on the other end.

▶ Do not put your present call on hold to take Call Waiting. The only exception is when you are expecting an important call, and you have already warned your first caller that you might have to jump ship if the other call comes in. But, in general, the purpose of Call Waiting is to keep your callers from getting a busy signal. With Call Waiting, they can dial once, leave you a message, and know that you'll return their call. It is considered rude to take Call Waiting while speaking to someone else.

▶ Don't indulge in small talk in a business call. You might have a couple of extra minutes, but the other person might not. And it's not professional. It's enough to bracket your business message with friendly bookends—one on either side:

"Dr. Mansfield, how are you? Not too busy, I hope? ... Thanks for your time, then. Good-bye!"

"Hello, Mary. I hope all's well with you and your family. Good-bye then, and give my best to Swithin."

"Leonard! How's it going? ... See you at the banquet."

"Ms. Rashid, good morning. Did your place survive the storm last night? ... Good-bye now! And don't forget to shut the windows tonight!"

▶ Multitasking is a way of life for many people, but it's disconcerting to be speaking with someone on the telephone and realize that they are stapling reports together or washing dishes or tapping away at their computer or shuffling papers and slamming file drawers. If you are really that busy, perhaps you could call the person later. Alternately, with someone you know well, you could ask, "Do you mind if I staple while we talk?"

Special Situations

▶ The telephone might already be one of your greatest time-savers. (In other contexts, it can be the opposite. These other contexts usually involve deadlines and high-pressure assignments.) But if it is not, make the telephone do the work of meetings and even conferences. Some people, most often extroverts, prefer meetings to telephones. But with the need to keep fighting trim in today's competitive business environment, you can save time, tempers, energy, and money by not having to move people around and by sidestepping the inevitable time-wasters that accompany in-person meetings. As Fran Lebowitz put it in a different context, "The telephone is a good way to talk to people without having to offer them a drink."

> *In almost every thriller, a point is reached when someone, usually calling from a phone booth, telephones with a vital piece of information, which he cannot divulge by phone. By the time the hero arrives at the place where they had arranged to meet, the caller is dead, or too near death to tell. There is never an explanation for the reluctance of the caller to impart his message in the first place.*
> —RENATA ADLER

▶ Occasionally, when you are in the middle of a telephone call, you might hear the person's other line ring persistently. You are not obliged to give up your time, but when you are able to do so, it is a wonderful relief to the other person if you will say something like: "I hear your other line." "Do you need to get that?" "I'll be glad to hold."

In a related situation, it is helpful when calling a place of business to begin by saying: "Are you helping a customer at the moment? If you are, I'll be glad to hold." This is actually more self-serving than it appears, for if the other person doesn't have to juggle two phone lines or a phone call and a customer, they are more likely to devote themselves to you and your query.

▶ You have probably discovered that the telephone is the best way to ask a favor of someone. You don't have to see the cloud pass over their face or watch their eyes slide sideways, foreshadowing their evasive answer. The telephone is all very well and good for those asking favors. But what about those being asked? If you are not quick on your mental feet, your answer must be:

"Do you need an answer right now? I'd rather call back after I've thought about it."

"Give me a couple of days to decide, will you?"

"Hmm, it might work, but I'm not sure. Let me call you later."

"I see I've got something on the calendar. Let me check that out first."

"Is it okay for me to get back to you? I can't say right now."

"It's been busy—let me make sure I have time before I say yes."

"Let me look at the calendar first. I'll call you tomorrow."

"May I call you back on that?"

"Naturally, I'd like to say yes, but ... here, I know, let me call you back."

"Thanks for the offer. Let me check my schedule and get back to you."

"You know I'd do anything for you, but this is going to be tricky. May I call you back?"

This will give you time to (a) make a decision about how to answer and (b) come up with a really good sentence saying that you can't. If you say "yes" to the request, remember that for the moment you have a certain power, so get your conditions in:

"Could we work it this way?"

"I could swing it if we..."

"I'd be glad to help, but I'm only free on..."

172   The Art of Talking to Anyone

"What I could do is…"

"What works for me is…"

- Because telephone conversations are, by their very nature, ephemeral, devise a system that works for you to take notes during a call. You might think you will remember what was said later in the day, but after six more phone calls and two meetings, it's not likely. If more than a name or a figure or two are mentioned, ask the other person to fax you a copy of the information. Don't hesitate to ask the person to repeat something or spell names. This shows that you are not only careful but that you respect the other person's information.

- What do you do about the conversation you can't have because the person will not return your call? First, ask yourself if someone else can supply the information. Second, consider that the only reason the person isn't returning the call is because they don't want to. Give up. Third, leave a clear message with a time deadline: "Gene, can you call me before 4:00 Wednesday afternoon?" If they don't respond, go back to "first."

- Cell phones are so ubiquitous now that they might be outnumbering us. Caveats regarding cell phones include: (1) Don't carry on a cell-phone conversation while you are checking out at the supermarket, paying for your dry cleaning, or otherwise dealing with a person standing in front of you. Cell-phone conversations with disembodied persons do not take precedence over interactions with embodied persons. In some cases, cell-phone users have taken rudeness to unexpected new levels. Make your calls before or after your encounters with friends, salespeople, etc. (2) Be sure the other person is as comfortable as you are with a phone conversation that takes place while you walk down Fifth Avenue in the midst of honking horns and raucous shouts or while you are driving and they wait through your near-misses and your mutterings at other drivers. Keep in mind that those kinds of calls are more convenient for you than they are for the other person. (3) Shut off your cell phone or set it to vibrate when you are in movie theaters, hospitals, houses of worship, classrooms, restaurants, or other venues where its ring would be disturbing.

Topics of Conversation

With personal phone calls, just about anything goes. (See Chapter 16 for tips on speaking with family and friends.) In a commercial call, there is only one topic: the question, issue, complaint, or order you're calling about. In a business call, little is usually said besides the business issue. But in certain contexts, a little phone talk does not come amiss after the business is taken care of. It should still be kept short.

Topics to Consider

Appreciation—if you can slip in a little congratulations or word of appreciation, do so

Article in that day's paper

Fitness

Hobby you have in common

Local-interest news

Movie or book recommendation

Mutual friend's illness, surgery, death

Restaurant, book, veterinarian, physician you want to recommend

Social or business event you are both invited to

Sports

Topical national or local event

Traffic or parking that affects both of you

Vacation or holidays—asking about

Weather

Work-related issues: favorite software, e-mail problems, helpful Internet sites

Topics to Avoid

Confidential matters

Controversial issues

Criticisms of others

Domestic complaints

Event to which the other wasn't invited

Failures

Gossip

How much things cost

Money

Negative comments about the workplace

Personal problems

Personal tidbits about others

Politics

Religion

Remarks about the other person's appearance, habits

Salaries—yours or theirs

Sex

Work problems that aren't yours to share

Your health

Conversation Starters

"Charlene, this is Louis. I'll be brief."

"Gene, this is Don with a quick question."

"Good afternoon, Walter. This is Joanna. May I have a minute of your time?"

"Good morning! Avery Gifford here. Are you free now, or shall I call back later?"

"Hello. This is Rhoda Courtney returning your call. Is this a good time for you?"

"Hello. This is Rose Lorimer speaking. Do you have a minute just now?"

"Hi, Demmie, this is Susan. I know you're busy, so this'll be quick."

"Hi! This is Art Bellairs calling. Is this a convenient time to speak with you?"

"Hi. This is Meg Kissock with the figures you wanted. I'll be glad to call back if you're busy just now."

"Hi! This is Sam Langden. I wanted to go over the Arnold Ainger report with you. Is this a good time for that?"

"Hi! This is Sue. Did I catch you in the middle of something?"

"Marian! Junior Bates here. I have a quick question for you. Are you free just now?"

"This is Barbara Molnar. Do you have a minute to discuss the dinner menu for the fundraiser?"

If They Say...You Say

It's up to you whether to go quickly to business or to spend a few minutes chatting. For the first, you give a one-word or a statement answer. For the second, you give your response and then ask a question. It depends on your goal. If you want to establish a connection with someone, you chat a little. If it's straight business, you don't.

If They Say	You Say
"Can I get back to you on that?"	"Of course! I'll need your answer by Thursday."
"Did I catch you at a bad time?"	"Actually, you did. What's a good time to call you back?"
"And so then she says to me..."	"Charlie? I've got a little situation here. Can we finish this conversation later?"
"Guess who!"	"I'm sorry. You must have the wrong number." [Hang up.]
"Well, finally! A real person. I hate getting an answering machine."	"Really."
"Beautiful weather we're having."	"Great! I understand you moved here from Alaska. How long did winter usually last there?"
"How's it going?"	"Actually, this is a great week. We finished remodeling the lobby. Take a look at it next time you're here."
"How's life treating you?"	"Great! Great! Listen, the figures you asked for are being faxed to you even as we speak."
"How about those Lakers?"	"What a game! Have you always been a fan, or has it been just since you moved here?"
"What a game last night!"	"Sure was! We could stand a few more like that. Say, do you know what's happening with our order?"
"Did you and your husband find a house?"	"Thanks for asking. We did and we're delighted. Do you have a lawn service you'd recommend?"

Closing Lines

In most circumstances, the person who makes the call is the one who ends it. And that can usually be done with a dispatch that barely qualifies as politeness.

"Bye."

"Catch you later."

"Cheerio!"

"Ciao!"

"Good-bye."

"I'll call when I know more. Bye."

"Let me know when you find out, will you?"

"Okay, that does it. Bye."

"See you later."

"So long."

"Take care."

"Thanks for your time, Sid. Bye."

"That'll do it, I guess. Thanks again!"

"That's exactly what I was looking for—thanks!"

"Well, I won't keep you. Bye."

"You've been a big help. Thanks."

CHAPTER 15

Talking With Anyone in Times of Trouble

> *People sinking into self-pity and depression are dreary, but they can't get out of it by themselves. So every now and then, just sit there and listen, and listen, and listen. You're paying your membership dues in the human race.*
>
> —BARBARA WALTERS

Introduction

You and a friend or co-worker are chatting about nothing in particular or walking down the street or waiting for the subway when abruptly the conversational weather turns from sunny to stormy. A divorce. Financial troubles. An illness in the family. The other person is hurting. And you need to say something.

Or you attend a wake, funeral, cremation, or interment. What do you say, how can you make small talk with the mourners? What do you say to the family of someone who committed suicide?

How do you make everyday conversation with someone who has a terminal illness? Or whose child has been arrested? Or who's been fired? Or who's going into or coming out of substance abuse treatment?

When other people's troubles touch your life—and it's hard to imagine a life that isn't touched at times—you'll want to have some appropriate responses on hand.

Conversations dealing with troubles are not "small talk," but that's where they often show up. You're skating along on pleasant conversational ice when suddenly a big crack opens up and you plunge into freezing waters. You can hardly say, "I thought we were just shooting the breeze here. I should probably get home."

People's troubles come in two forms: troubles that blindside them through no fault of their own (deaths in the family, being laid off, assaults, burglaries, car accidents, fires) and troubles in which they have played a big or small role (having troubles with the neighbors, complaints about work, disagreements and conflicts with friends or family, troubles at work, debts).

In the first instance, you give all you can afford to give of your sympathetic ear and a few low-key reflections on what they tell you they're feeling.

In the second instance, being a good friend might involve the foregoing plus some clarifying questions. Sometimes people make trouble for themselves over and over again. It's a long shot, but once in a great while your not-too-pointed questions might turn on a lightbulb in their head.

> *Those who are unhappy have no need for anything in this world but people capable of giving them their attention.*
> —SIMONE WEIL

It is usually from this second group that sometimes comes a request for financial or other help. They might want you to intercede for them with a spouse or a boss, to run interference for them with an angry neighbor, or to lend them enough for this month's rent. Because you believe that help in this situation is only a Band Aid for the larger problem or because you are not able to supply what's needed, you might be in the awkward position of saying "no" to a friend caught up in misfortune. They feel you could bail them out. You don't think so. What do you say?

With your own common sense and compassion plus a little inspiration from the suggestions below, you can prove yourself a friend indeed, a friend in need.

Do's

▶ Let the other person talk as much as they want. Fill in with sympathetic, understanding murmurs, but don't offer suggestions, help, or advice at this point. Statements from you are only an interruption in the story they're trying to tell themselves. Let them tell it. Over and over again, if necessary.

▶ Vary your responses, if you can: "Oh no." "How awful for you." "Ouch." "I'm so sorry." "Dear me." "Good grief." "What a situation." "Don't tell me..."

▶ Sometimes silence is a good response. When people broach a sad subject with you, they want to tell it. In most cases, you don't have to say a word of encouragement; the story will unfold to the end, or to as much of an end as it has.

Silence—if you are also paying attention to the person and showing this by focusing on them and looking as sympathetic as you can—is as healing as anything you can say or do. Silence also makes the person bring forth that next bit, and the next, and the next.

> *Sometimes being a friend means mastering the art of timing. There is a time for silence. A time to let go and allow people to hurl themselves into their own destiny. And a time to prepare to pick up the pieces when it's all over.*
> —GLORIA NAYLOR

▶ If the matter is confidential, assure the other person that the news will go no further.

▶ Show your appreciation for the person as someone who can meet the challenges and griefs of the situation. You might say things like:

"I believe in you. You will come out on the other side of this."

"I can't imagine anything worse, but I know you will sort it out bit by bit."

"I know you can handle this."

"I'm impressed with how clearly you're seeing the situation."

"I wish you didn't have to deal with this, but you will get through it."

"The steps you've already taken are really sound."

"You have a good grip on things, and I know you're going to be all right."

▶ Try to hear and respond to the feelings underneath: desperation, grief, confusion, panic, hopelessness, anxiety. When a person is in trouble, the feelings are all going to be negative feelings, but watch for the kind of total despair that sometimes precedes suicidal thoughts.

▶ Ask questions, being careful that they are not accusatory ("How *could* you?") or intrusive ("Have you been crying a lot?"). In the case of a death, you can ask about the deceased—where and how they died, what they were like, when the person last saw them. In the case of trouble, ask neutral questions that might help the person see their situation in a new way: "Who can help with this?" "What can you do about it?" "Have you notified anyone yet?" "How are you thinking you can solve this?" "What did Robin have to say about it?" "Is this the worst thing that could have ever happened to you, or is it a medium-size blow, or is it something that you won't even think about a month from now?"

Don'ts

- Don't say you understand how the other person feels. First, you can't possibly understand because you're not in the precise, exact same situation ("similar" doesn't cut it). Second, the other person will, at some level, resent this.

- Don't fake sympathy or understanding. Even lost in their own troubles, people will notice empty responses. If you're not feeling particularly empathetic but want to support the person, give them a hug and make arrangements to talk more about it later when you can bring a little more acceptance to the conversation.

> *Nothing can get people to take on and solve their own problems faster than a good question.*
> —Dorothy Leeds

- Whether it's a death or a loss or bankruptcy or even something that you consider insignificant, don't tell the other person not to think about it, and don't try to change the subject. They need to say their piece, sometimes over and over. Getting them to change the subject is often more for your comfort than theirs, because nothing will stop them from thinking about it.

> *Someone to tell it to is one of the fundamental needs of human beings.*
> —Miles Franklin

- Don't use words that inflate or overly dramatize the situation: "tragic," "catastrophic," "heinous," "worst thing I ever heard of." Use, instead, synonyms for words the other person is using to describe how they feel.

- Don't emphasize your own feelings over theirs: "I couldn't sleep a wink last night thinking about you" or "I've been so upset!" It's good to let them know you feel bad, but the greater grief and the superlatives in the way of feelings are theirs. Some egocentric people see everything through the prism of their own lives. It takes away something from the troubled person when it sounds as though you are suffering even more than they are.

- Do not offer troubled people philosophical adages, clichés, religious pieties, simplistic explanations, "meanings" to be found in the event, or announcements of God's intentions, involvement, or directions. If you and the other person share spiritual ideas, it might be helpful. For most people in trouble, however, there appears to be no comfort anywhere, and it is irritating to have others try to soothe them with words that appear irrelevant or inappropriate to their situation.

▶ Depending on the kind of trouble your friend is in, do not try to teach them a lesson, lecture them, label their behavior, moralize, advise them, or otherwise try to change them. Change comes only from the inside out. It's not even that such "help" is irritating and inappropriate; it is completely counterproductive.

▶ Don't confuse "my condolences" (which are offered only in the event of a death) with "my sympathy" (which is used for a death, but can also be offered to those who have suffered from a fire, flood, storm, or natural disaster; burglary, theft, or violent crime; a lost job, bankruptcy, personal reverses, or other misfortunes).

Special Situations

▶ In the case of a death, the most comforting words you can say to the mourners closest to the deceased (besides "I'm so sorry") are stories, anecdotes, memories, or incidents about the deceased person—how you met them, their influence on your life, a funny thing they said, how they loved their family, how much they will be missed.

▶ Events following a death—funerals, wakes, cremations, burials, and memorial services—are possibly one of the most difficult places to make conversation. People tend to stand around and talk either before or after such events, and you need to contribute something. Because the only real topic of conversation possible is the deceased and their survivors, you might say things like:

"After my father died, your brother used to call me at college once a week. You can't imagine what that meant to me."

"Did you know that she visited prisoners at the county jail every Tuesday night?"

"Even after losing his wife and son, he refused to become bitter or despondent, but remained generous and loving."

"He used to do dental work for people who didn't have insurance and then he'd 'forget' to bill them."

"I think there are probably dozens of people who all think she was their best friend. She made you feel like that."

"She's the one who started the birthday club. I don't know how we can keep getting together without her."

"Two days before she died, she was still telling jokes."

"You know, he was being treated for this for years, but I don't think anyone even knew it."

- ▶ Miscarriages and stillbirths are still not regarded as the profound tragedy that they are. Remember to give the same sympathy to those who've lost a child that way as you would to any other grieving parent. Don't say: "You already have two lovely children—be grateful for what you have" or "You're young yet—you can try again." And the worst of all: "Don't feel so bad. After all, it isn't as though you lost a *child*." They have lost a child.

- ▶ The death of a pet or companion animal is a serious blow. Whether you can understand this kind of attachment or not, respond at the level of the person suffering the loss. If they are devastated, you are devastated for them. Remember in the weeks afterwards to ask how they're doing, and to mention the animal's name, along with any stories you recall about it.

- ▶ When someone you work with dies, conversations for weeks afterwards carry the weight of that loss. No matter what people are saying out loud, most are thinking—at least occasionally—about the missing person. It helps to continue talking to those who were closest to the person about their missing friend. To not ever be mentioned is a second, smaller kind of death. Survivors are comforted—not inspired to new heights of grief—by talking about the person.

> *To mention a loved object, a person, or a place to someone else is to invest that object with reality.*
> —ANNE MORROW LINDBERGH

- ▶ In the case of a suicide, offer your sympathy as you would to any bereaved family. Because many survivors experience feelings of guilt, rejection, confusion, and social stigma, they need to know that you are thinking of them, that you care. Although it is generally appropriate to say you were "shocked to hear about" someone's death, avoid the phrase in this case. Don't ask questions, speculate about how the death could have been prevented, or dwell on the fact of the suicide; what matters is that the person is gone and the family is grieving. Instead, talk about how the person touched your life, share a happy memory, or express sympathy for the bereaved's pain.

- ▶ Saying "no" to someone in trouble is a disagreeable challenge. You might have to refuse a loan because either you know it will only prolong the other person's problems or because you do not have the money. Because it's family or a friend or possibly even an acquaintance who has turned to you in desperation, you'll want to be kind, tactful, and firm.

When turning down such a request, phrase it in terms of an inability of yours (an I-statement: "I don't have the money") rather than a character flaw of theirs (a you-statement, such as "You know you won't repay this").

It also helps if you first give your excuse, and then your refusal ("I'm going to be away that weekend, so I won't be able to help you"). And then, the real secret to making a refusal stick is to repeat it ad nauseum. Don't even change your wording and, whatever you do, don't start offering one reason after another. The other person will argue it down, forcing you to give another reason, which they will also prove worthless. Simply repeat the line you have chosen until it finally is accepted by the other person. Don't make a decision sound negotiable if it is not. It is kinder to be clear that the answer is no. You might say something like:

"After careful thought, I've decided I can't help this time, but I certainly wish you the best."

"I am sorry to disappoint you, but I can't in all conscience do that."

"I'd like to help you, but I can't."

"I'd like to say 'yes,' but it's not on the cards."

"I don't feel comfortable lying about this."

"I hope you can make other arrangements because we aren't able to lend you anything."

"I hope you will accept both my good wishes and my inability to help out—and, no, it's not negotiable. There's no point in discussing it further."

"I'm not bonded, and you'll need someone who is."

"I'm overextended at the moment. Maybe you could try someone else."

"I'm sorry, but having you and your family live with us is out of the question."

"I'm sorry, but I simply cannot."

"I'm sorry I can't explain my decision, but the answer is no."

"I truly sympathize with your request and wish I could help, but I can't."

"It's not possible, Jennifer."

Talking With Anyone in Times of Trouble

"It's really hard for me to turn you down. I hope you can find some other solution."

"I've decided I can't, for personal reasons."

"I've taken on more than I can handle recently. I'm sorry."

"I wish I could, but I can't."

"I wish I could help, but it's not possible just now."

"I wish I didn't have to refuse you, Sarah, but I cannot see my way to making you a loan at this time."

"I would normally be happy to help, but we are in debt ourselves."

"My answer has to be negative and I'd rather not share my reasons, if you don't mind."

"My work schedule is absolutely inflexible at the moment. I hope you can find someone else to watch Sammy during the day."

"Sorry, I don't think that would be a good thing for me to do."

"Thank you for asking, but no."

"Under normal circumstance, I'd be happy to help you, but..."

"Unfortunately, your request comes at a particularly difficult time for me."

"We aren't in a position to help you."

"We've maxed out our home equity loan, so we won't be able to help you."

"You can imagine my dilemma, but it's not do-able."

"You know I am sympathetic to your situation, but I'm simply not able to help out."

"You know I hate to refuse you, but I have to."

Topics of Conversation

Once you know another person is worried or grieving or upset, the choice of topics is limited. You can hardly speak of trivia when they are so obviously suffering.

Your conversation is going to revolve around the problem and its attendant practical considerations: arranging a ride to work, listing phone calls that need to be made, checking out available resources, letting others know about the situation, making appointments with counselors, lawyers, realtors, temporary employment agencies, physicians, and others who might be of assistance.

Conversation Starters

The other person has opened the line of conversation about trouble, grief, or unhappy events, so you will be responding to their remarks rather than starting new topics yourself.

Helpful Things to Say

"Do you have family nearby?"

"I can't imagine how you must feel."

"I can't imagine what you're going through."

"I don't know what to say."

"I'll be glad to take over your work at the office while you tend to this."

"I'll keep you in my thoughts and prayers."

"I'm so sorry about this."

"I'm truly sorry to hear about your loss."

*You may choose your word like a connoisseur,
And polish it up with art,
But the word that sways, and stirs, and stays,
Is the word that comes from the heart.*
—ELLA WHEELER WILCOX

"Is there anything I can do? I am quite sincere about helping."

"Let me be responsible for your customers while you're taking time off to deal with this."

"This is a terrible loss for you."

"You absolutely must stay with us until you find out how much of the house was saved."

"You have all my sympathy."

Unfortunate Things to Say

"At least she is out of her misery and isn't suffering anymore."

"At least you had him for eighteen years."

"Be happy for what you had."

"Be thankful you have another child."

"Don't cry. Things will look better tomorrow."

"God never makes a mistake."

"God only sends burdens to those who can handle them."

"He's in a better place now."
"He was old and had a good life."
"I don't know how you can stand it."
"I feel almost worse than you do about this."
"If you can keep busy, you'll soon forget."
"I have a friend who's going through the same thing."
"I heard you're not taking it well."
"I'm sure God had a purpose in sending you this burden."
"It's a blessing in disguise."
"It's just as well you never got to know the baby."
"It's probably better this way. Every cloud has a silver lining, you know."
"It's probably good that he died when he did; otherwise he might have been a vegetable."
"Keep your chin up."
"Life is for the living."
"Life must go on—you'll feel better before you know it."
"Oh, I know exactly how you feel."
"Perhaps it was for the best—there might have been something wrong with the baby. This was nature's way of taking care of it."
"She is much better off now."
"Time heals all wounds."
"Why didn't you call me the minute it happened?"
"You have to be brave for your family."
"You know, you're not the first person this has happened to."
"You'll get over it."
"You must get on with your life."
"You're still young; you can always marry again."
"You should have divorced him a long time ago."

If They Say...You Say

Notice the pattern below where you respond with something sympathetic, and then add a question to keep the conversation going.

If They Say	You Say
"But what should I do?"	"You've already mentioned some options, and I'm certain you will make an excellent decision. What are you going to do today?"
"And then, I don't know…"	"Tell me more. What was your first thought when you heard?"
"My family doesn't even want to talk with me."	"Hmm. So what are you going to do next?"
"I just heard that my mother died."	"Oh no! I'm so sorry to hear that. When did this happen?"
"I am devastated. I hardly know where to turn."	"Yes, and why wouldn't you be devastated? I wonder…have you spoken with Rabbi Epstein? He always has something helpful to say."
"You have to help me!"	"Let's make a list here of what needs to be done. Have you done that?"
"You're the only one who can help!"	"Well, let's see. Have you talked with anyone else yet?"
"There simply is no reason to go on living."	"I'd like to come over tonight and talk with you and Pat—will you be home?"

Closing Lines

"All will be well—not for some time, but eventually—so hang onto that thought."

"Call me, day or night, if you think of anything else I can do."

"Do one small nice thing for yourself tonight, will you?"

"I hope there's a happy ending for this story. I believe there is."

"I hope your many good memories will be of some comfort to you in the difficult days ahead."

"I'll be thinking about you."

"I'm glad you told me. Let's talk again tomorrow."

"Keep in touch, will you? I'll call next week to see how you're doing."

"Let me know how things turn out, will you?"

"You've met other challenges. You're going to meet this one."

CHAPTER 16

Talking With Family and Friends

> *The etiquette of intimacy is very different from the etiquette of formality, but manners are not just something to show off to the outside world. If you offend the head waiter, you can always go to another restaurant. If you offend the person you live with, it's very cumbersome to switch to a different family.*
>
> —Judith Martin

Introduction

At first glance, it would seem that most people know how to converse with family and friends. However, that assumption, and the familiarities that accompany it, account for some less-than-stellar conversations among family members and between friends.

It is, in fact, more difficult to remain mannerly with our nearest and dearest because we take them for granted. And, to be fair, they take us for granted too. They don't shower us with the admiring glances and the hearty laughter that co-workers and new acquaintances do (because they don't have to live with us), and we, in turn, don't laugh as hard or share flirting looks and appreciative comments with family and friends. What comes around goes around.

> *It is so easy to be full of conversation, of amusement, when you are dealing with people whom you far more seldom meet; but at home, to be alive, to be amusing, to be full of new subjects for conversation—that is a demand upon human nature to which human nature with growing feebleness responds.*
>
> —Bede Jarrett

However, nothing pays off as well in terms of happiness and life satisfaction as cultivating the love and goodwill of friends and family through the gracious conversations of equals.

Do's

- Exert yourself to treat family and friends as you would a valued client or the CEO of your company or the surgeon who's going to operate on you. We are sometimes nicer to everyone we meet in a day than we are to family when we arrive home at night. It's not that we are actively unpleasant. We commit those sins of omission that pass almost unnoticed: the little compliment not given, the failure to tousle a head or pat a shoulder, the kiss that never leaves your lips, the lack of a touch that says, "I see you."

- Show your appreciation. Never worry about whether you already told the person you enjoyed the home-grown eggplant or liked the job they did on the back porch—we never tire of hearing compliments. Don't wait for big events like graduations and weddings and new homes to let people know you think they're terrific. Lowering a golf score, edging the lawn, making a special dessert, getting a good-looking haircut—anything will serve to let others know that you notice and appreciate them.

- When you find yourself with family or friends, edge into the conversation by listening for the primary feelings of the other person. Do they seem happy, contented, disappointed, discouraged, angry, worried, excited, sad, uncomfortable? Respond to the feelings you're picking up. This doesn't mean that you become worried or excited or disappointed, but you do not launch into a happy story of your most recent success if the other person is anxious and unhappy.

    Let them tell you what's happening in their life, and try to isolate the item that might be responsible for the mood you're seeing. A person might talk about a shopping trip, a letter from someone, phone calls from friends, and what they're having for dinner. But their voice changes when they mention the letter. You'll want to ask about it.

> *To be polite to everybody except the people they love most is a nervous affectation that afflicts many families...when they come home, they take off their smiles and soft words, and sit about, spiritually in their underwear. This isn't pretty.*
> —MARGARET FISHBACK

On the other hand, if the person is upbeat and elated about good news, try to share their joy even if your own day hasn't been all sunshine. If the other person is sensitive to the nuances in conversational back-and-forthing, they'll pick up on your mood, and by the end of the conversation you will both have found much satisfaction in your talk with each other.

▶ Ask questions about the other person's life without, however, sounding like a prosecutor or muckraker. A simple "What have you been doing lately?" or "How was your day?" (and then really listening) is enough to start a conversation. If you should get in reply, "Oh, not much" or "Nothing really," narrow the question to something specific: "Whatever happened to that paper you were writing?" or "Weren't you planning to go to Sicily this year?" or "Weren't you looking at used cars the last time we talked?"

▶ While asking questions, however, respect others' privacy. Just because you know each other well does not mean you are entitled to their every thought.

▶ Be tactful. Too many people think they can "let it all hang out" when they are among family and friends. Act as if this friend is your supervisor ... or royalty.

▶ Listen carefully, and listen not only to the words but to the feelings underneath. Listening is the single most effective way of making and keeping friends. Listening doesn't mean not saying anything. Certain ways of listening tell the other person you hear them, you treasure them, and you support them. (See Chapter 3 on listening.)

Hearing the words isn't enough ("James and I spent last weekend in San Francisco"). What is the feeling behind the words? Delight with the weekend? Bewilderment because it didn't turn out as expected? Anxiety because this is not something the person ordinarily does?

There was a definite process by which one made people into friends, and it involved talking to them and listening to them for hours at a time.
—Rebecca West

In a good conversation both people need to be reacting to the same feelings. Even if nothing is said overtly ("You sound pretty disappointed"), if you respond at the correct feeling level ("So," rather than "Hey, terrific! I like James!"), the other person feels heard.

Talking With Family and Friends

- Share your feelings. Not all your feelings. Not all the time. But family and friends are there to support you, and they can best do this if they know what's going on with you. Psychologically, other people are drawn to sharing their feelings when you share yours.

> *A deadness occurs in relationships when people are no longer willing to tell each other how they really feel.*
> —Shakti Gawain

- Elaborate. When you are answering a question or telling something, bring in details, specific descriptions, colorful words. This doesn't necessarily mean to speak at such length that all about you people are falling off couches and chairs. But where a simple "yes" or "no" will stall out a conversation, a "Yes, and then ..." with a story will usually keep it going.

- Don't wait for the big events, the big feelings, and the big ideas to make conversation, convey appreciation, and build relationships. It's the everyday sharing that binds people together.

- Mine the past for material if you can't think of anything else to talk about. Most people can tell any number of stories about where they've been to an interested listener. The listener's reward is to leave knowing that the other person thinks they are handsome, brilliant, and rich besides. It's even more effective to talk about shared memories.

- When you're stuck for conversation because, after all, you've known this person for years, ask a "What if...?" question. Their answers might surprise you ... and them. Some people love this kind of mental speculation; others are impatient with it. Don't press if the person doesn't seem interested. If they are, however, try asking something like:

> *We shared everything all our lives, the important ones and the trivial ones, and it's the trivial ones that build ties between people.*
> —Rae Foley

"What if you could buy one thing right now? What would it be?"

"What if you could change one thing about the United States or about the world? What would it be?"

"What if you could change one thing in your past? What would it be?"

"What if you could invite any person in the world to spend a weekend at your house? Who would it be?"

"What if you could know your whole future? Would you want to?"

"What if you could speak one foreign language? What would it be and why would you choose it?"

"What if you had a million dollars to spend in the next week? What would you do with it?"

"What if you had another life to live? Who would you be?"

"What if you had three wishes that would come true? What would you wish for?"

> *A relationship isn't meant to be an insurance policy, a life preserver, or a security blanket.*
> —DIANE CROWLEY

"What if you won a ticket to fly anywhere in the world? Where would you go?"

Other thought-provoking, imaginative questions might lead to interesting conversations:

"Are you planning a vacation for any time in the next couple of years?"

"Did you ever consider going into politics?"

"Did your mother or father ever say anything wise to you that has remained with you all these years?"

"Do you believe in coincidence? In ESP? In palm-reading? In astrology? In fortune telling? In ghosts?"

"Do you have a business philosophy? Or a personal philosophy?"

"Have you ever thought about going to a séance?"

"How did you get interested in genealogy?"

"How did you manage as a single mom with three small children? I didn't know you then and I've always wondered."

"What advice would you give to someone graduating from college?"

"What are you looking forward to these days?"

"What are your pet peeves about people? What kind of people drive you crazy?"

"What does this music remind you of?"

"What do you most like to do on a rainy day?"

"What do you remember most vividly about your childhood?"

"Whatever happened to your wanting to be a painter?"

"What is the most boring situation you can possibly imagine?"

"What started you collecting spoons?"

"When did you first know that you wanted to go into business?"

"Who are your heroes?"

▶ Into every life some rain must fall; you might experience disagreements or bad feelings between you and others. Learn the many uses and advantages of the heartfelt apology. With friends and family, it might be one of your best relationship-building tools. Bad apologies like a short-tempered, angry "I'm sorry! I said I was sorry!" rarely mend fences. To restore peace to your friendship, try an apology like:

"How can I make this right with you?"

"I agree; I was incredibly inconsiderate."

"I am so sorry."

"I clearly wasn't thinking."

"I don't know what possessed me."

"I hope you can forgive me."

"I'm as mad at me as you are."

"I'm not surprised you're upset. I would be too."

"I owe you an apology."

"I was wrong. Dead wrong."

"That was thoughtless of me."

"There's absolutely no excuse for it."

"This will not happen again, I promise you."

"What a mindless thing for me to do."

"You're right when you say sometimes I don't really listen to you."

Don'ts

▶ Do not offer solutions or advice when someone is telling you about their problems. The only time you suggest a solution or give advice is after being asked specifically, repeatedly, and sincerely. The reason for this is that listening with your whole attention is far more likely to help people solve their problems.

If you are skilled at this, you might ask clarifying questions. A clarifying question is not: "What on earth were you thinking?" or "You did *what*?" or "Why would you do something like that?" Examples of questions that help people look at their problems more clearly might be:

> *Among the most disheartening and dangerous of... advisors, you will often find those closest to you, your dearest friends, members of your own family, perhaps, loving, anxious, and knowing nothing whatever.*
> —MINNIE MADDERN FISKE

"Are you excited about that?"

"Does that bother you?"

"Have you ever done that before?"

"How do you feel about saying 'maybe' instead of 'no'?"

"If you had a choice, would you go or stay?"

"Were you hoping to be invited to go along?"

"What do you think they want in return?"

"Which do you need the most?"

"Would you feel more relieved or more disappointed if the deal fell through?"

"Would you prefer not to be moved to the other building?"

▶ Even family and friends have their limits. Try not to monopolize the conversation or to insist on talking about a topic long after everyone else has lost interest.

Be aware of people trying to change the subject, of a dearth of interested questions, of wandering eyes and suppressed yawns. (See Chapter 8 for more on monopolizing the conversation.)

> *There is hardly a company that will not tire of the sustained discussion of one subject, no matter how interesting it may be.*
> —LILLIAN EICHLER

▶ Don't give one-word answers: "Do you want some coffee?" "No." Better to tack on something to keep the conversation going: "No. I don't do caffeine at all any more. Are you still drinking two pots of coffee a day?" The other person could reply, "Yes." But it's better to link another thought to it: "Yes, but it doesn't bother me. Was the caffeine getting to you? Why did you quit?" The idea is to make a daisy chain of thoughts, one linking to the next.

- Don't give up on people when conversation is difficult. We don't have enough family and friends in this world to be able to write off some of them. Don't push it when talk doesn't flow smoothly, and try again another day.

Special Situations

- Arguments and discussions can be distinguished by the degree of heat that accompanies them. Discussions are usually cerebral, dispassionate, and low-key. Arguments are emotional, intense, and anything but low-key. They can lead to bad feelings and disruptions of relationships. Marion Dane Bauer said, "I was an adult before I began to learn that there is a difference between a conversation and an argument."

Avoidance is an effective strategy most of the time. If a conversation looks as if it's about to turn contentious, back down if you can, change the subject, or leave the room.

Choose your battles. Arguments are a necessary part of life, but they should be fairly few and far between.

The expression "to pick a fight" is based in reality; some individuals seem to feel most alive when they are arguing. The best response in this case is simply to refuse to be engaged. No matter what they say, respond with nods, shrugs, indecipherable grunts, or "um"s. The more persistently they challenge you, the quieter you become. It takes two to tango, and after a while they will tire of their one-person rant.

> *We didn't have a relationship; we had a personality clash.*
> —ALICE MOLLOY

Topics of Conversation

Perhaps some people have a constant fund of conversational topics when they are with family and friends. Their well evidently never runs dry. But they are not numerous, these conversational giants. And they do not seem to belong to *our* family. Sometimes we have to work a little at finding that next idea to share or a good question to ask when familiarity deadens us to the possibility of some truly good conversation. Try some of the topics below when you can't think of anything new to say.

Topics to Consider

Anecdotes, opinions, observations

A new or used item you or they just bought

Appreciation and congratulations—little things and big

Books: favorites, recently read, books read more than once, favorites from childhood

Changes in their house or yours or wherever you're meeting

Current enthusiasms and projects

Favorites: restaurant, meal, vacation, gadget, movie, animal, TV show, music, actor

Food: what's being served, favorites, recipes

Gardening—if it's of interest to you both

Hobbies or collections

Issues of shared interest: gun control, taxes, coming election, violence in society, the effect of advertising on young people, the environment

Jokes

Movies, plays, or television shows you or they have seen

News of family or friends that one of you doesn't know yet

Newspaper items of interest to you both

Occasion or reason that brings you together

Pets, if you both have them

Plans for the next week, next season, next year

Something that made you laugh recently

Sports you or they have played or watched

The arts, if this is a shared interest

Weather in your area, how it has affected either of you

What you and they have been doing lately

Work changes, news, items of interest

Topics to Avoid

Advice: what they ought to do

Bragging or putting down others

Criticisms of other family members or friends

Health, illnesses—unless you know there is a sincere interest in your situation

Money—what you or they make, what things cost, the depressing national economy

Off-color jokes, unless you know they are welcome

Other people's love lives—walk softly here

Personal problems and revelations that make others uncomfortable

Political and social issues that you disagree on

Religion, unless your beliefs are shared

Secrets or confidential matters involving other people

Sex

Telling the plots of books, movies, or TV shows

Work problems that aren't of interest to the others

> *Almost everyone is uncomfortable talking about money.*
> —OLIVIA MELLAN

Conversation Starters

"A lot's happened in your life since I last saw you. Start talking!"

"Do you ever look fit!"

"First let me see pictures of the baby."

"Good to see you!"

"How was your summer?"

"I've missed you!"

"Look what you've done to the living room—it's wonderful!"

"Remember the time we were supposed to meet at 8:00, and I thought you meant morning and you thought I meant night?"

"So what was your day like today?"

"Tell me everything about your trip to Atlanta."

> *Communication with another person—wasn't it the realest thing in life?*
> —ANNE MORROW LINDBERGH

"Whatever happened to your friend the juggler?"

"What have you been doing for fun lately?"

"What's new?"

"Where did you get the tan?"

"Who's the new neighbor?"

"Why don't we get together more often? It's always such a treat."

"You've never really told me what you do all day—and I'd like to hear about it."

If They Say...You Say

The conversation game with family and friends is usually lively. You can do your part to keep it that way by hitting the ball back in the other person's court, usually with a question attached, so that they have to return it to you. In this back-and-forthing, large and small life events are shared, as well as positive feelings.

If They Say	You Say
"There's not much new around here."	"I'll bet you've read six interesting books lately. Come on, tell me about them."
"I'm fine. How about you?"	"Funny you should ask, because I had an odd adventure last week that you'll like."
"Do you remember Pat Freeling?"	"No. Who was he?"
"Have you found any new fishing lures for your collection?	"As a matter of fact, I found my most unusual one of all just last week. I'll tell you about it if you tell me about your latest miniature tea set."
"I'm afraid to ask, but is the job getting any more pleasant?"	"Nope. I'm not sure what to do about it. I have three choices. Tell me what you think."
"What have you done to this office?"	"Thanks for asking! I got so tired of trying to stay organized in here. Let me show you..."
"I heard that your mother died. Do you feel like talking about it?"	"Actually I like to talk about her. About three months ago, she called..."

Closing Lines

"Bye for now."

"Hey, this was great!"

"I always enjoy seeing you. I wish we didn't live so far apart."

"I always have clean sheets on the guest room bed—come check them out!"

"I'll call next Tuesday to see what you found out at the doctor's."

"I'll stop by again next week."

"I love you!"

"Let me know how you make out with the lawyer."

"Next time we'll do this at my house."

"Nobody sets a table as well as you do—I'll be back soon!"

"See you soon!"

"Thanks for making the evening so special."

"Write and tell me how your finals go, OK?"

"You are dear to me. Be well!"

CHAPTER 17

Talking With Romance in Mind

Remember my unalterable maxim, where we love, we have always something to say.

—Lady Mary Wortley Montagu

Introduction

Most of us want to find and eventually pledge ourselves to that one person out of all the world who can make the sun shine and our hearts sing.

But meeting someone and falling in love is not all kisses and moonlight. There is, first, conversation. We have to actually speak with someone who is near enough to hear us but, as our suddenly humble heart tells us, as far away and unreachable as the stars.

When doubts and weak nerves attack, remember this: your future with this person depends on chemistry, luck, timing, circumstances, and, yes, even destiny. All you have to do is not get in the way.

> *Ultimately the bond of all companionship, whether in marriage or in friendship, is conversation.*
> —Oscar Wilde

Don't worry about being the best-looking, smartest, most creative, sharpest single on the block. The other person—if it's the right person—is looking for you, the real you, not some altered, hyped-up, artificial construct. So relax, observe a few guidelines, and prepare for the biggest adventure of your life.

Do's

- Begin slowly. Attune your conversational rhythm, intensity, and subject matter to the other person's. If they project a cool demeanor, yours should also be cool, casual, relaxed. If they project warmth, you can do likewise. You don't want to be false to who you are, but everyone has a range of emotional temperatures. In the beginning, find one that matches theirs.

- Conversation between two people with a little chemistry should be a teeter-totter process: first one person asks questions and shares some personal reflections, then the other person shares some personal reflections and asks questions. One person's questions and reflections trigger the other person's. If you're doing all the talking, something's not working. If one of you asks many questions but never volunteers any revealing information, something's not working.

> *Pleasant words are the food of love.*
> —OVID

- Self-revelation is key to building a relationship, but it's best to start small and lighthearted and build to bigger issues and more deeply held opinions. The other person wants to know more about you, so tell what you've been doing, feeling, thinking (not all at once, of course). This kind of self-revelation tends to elicit similar revelations from the other person. If it doesn't, ask questions to level the mutual revelations.

> *Talking to you is only thinking to myself—made easier.*
> —JOHN OLIVER HOBBES

- In the first few hours or days of a relationship, you are brief, you do not reveal as much as you will later (if there is a later), and you try to retain some emotional distance. You might, for example, relate a humorous incident from work, but you wouldn't describe a scene from your childhood with deep meaning for you. You wouldn't invite the other person to your family's home for dinner, but you might mention where your parents live and what they do. Be willing to accept a warm-up period until you are both on the same wavelength. Until then, rushing fences will probably hurt your cause.

- Use the other person's name now and then. There's nothing quite so wonderful as our name said by someone we're interested in.

- This is your chance to—let's bring back an old-fashioned term—court someone. You can woo with actions, but your conversation can also be a courting. Tell what you like about the other person. Be specific and detailed.

- Appreciation is always, well, appreciated, but it's a tricky art in the beginning of a relationship. While you could compliment someone's dancing, laugh at their jokes, or agree with their ideas, beyond that lie monsters. Commenting on a person's looks, dress, or behavior could be construed as intrusive or as coming on too fast. Commenting on their intelligence or appearing to evaluate their remarks with your approval sounds patronizing.

- You have two choices about conversational topics. The safe choice is to stay with generic subjects and lightly held views. This will give you a chance to see if there are any viable sparks between you before you have your first argument. On the other hand, being open about your politics or spiritual beliefs or likes and dislikes will let the other person know that you have fire in your belly. Whether it's their kind of fire or not will also be useful to know.

- Determine the other person's degree of interest in you, and accommodate yourself to it. If you feel you've been struck by lightning, but the other person appears far too calm to have experienced anything similar, adjust to their emotional level. You'll need patience while waiting either for lightning to strike them or for you decide that it never will.

  Watch for signs that your feelings are reciprocated. The sooner you know, the sooner you can make your choices.

  How can you tell if things are going well? Someone who asks you questions about yourself is most likely interested in you (or possibly a nervous conversationalist). If they don't ask any questions about you within the first fifteen minutes of meeting you, it's probably not a good sign.

  Once you see that you aren't the other person's cup of tea, move on; social stalkers are neither a popular nor a happy breed. You simply cannot make someone love you. So cut your losses and find that person who's looking for someone like you.

  Another indication of the other person's interest is what their eyes are doing. Someone truly taken with you will either hardly be able to look away from you or, if shy, will keep darting looks at you. The person who is indifferent to you will be searching the room to see who else is there, who might be more interesting.

A good way to get to know someone, or to get a shy person to talk more, is to ask "What if...?" questions:

"What if you and I were animals—what kind would we be?"

"What if you could have three wishes right now—what would you wish for?"

"What if you could invite any four people to dinner—whom would you invite?"

"What if you could learn to play any musical instrument—which one would you choose?"

"What if you could live during any time in history—which period would you choose?"

"What if you could marry any person who's ever lived—whom would you choose?"

"What if you could spend a month in any place in the world—where would you go?"

"What if your apartment were on fire—what would you grab on your way out?"

"What if you unexpectedly had $50,000—what would you do with it?"

"What if you were a politician—what top three issues would you work on?"

"What if you were a writer—what kind of book would you write?"

"What if you were independently wealthy and didn't have to work—what would you do with your time?"

Don'ts

▶ Don't ask about the other person's dating history, either directly or indirectly. This is off-putting; the other person will let you know anything you should know. Later on, the subject is more appropriate. Equally off-putting is mentioning other dates you've had, in an attempt to show how popular you are.

▶ Avoid the too-broad and largely unproductive "Tell me about yourself." Most people hardly know where to start, stammering and looking awkward. Those who dive right in, starting with the day they were born, will have put you to sleep by the time they get to their high school years. Ask instead narrower, somewhat impersonal questions: "Do you live in the neighborhood?" The talk then can range from a deli you both like to a movie one of you has seen at the Art Deco theater down the block to the new tennis courts in the park.

- Don't answer your cell phone when you're with the other person. Unless you are expecting an important call, and have explained this beforehand, the phone should not interrupt your time together.

- Don't try to be someone you aren't. Be on your best behavior, of course, but don't use language or gestures or actions that are not natural to you. The other person will sense that something is awry. They also might fall in love with someone who doesn't exist.

- Don't ask, "Are you free Friday tonight?" when calling for a first or second date. At this point, the other person might or might not want to see you, or they might be waiting to see what you had in mind and your question puts them on the spot. Offer instead a specific suggestion before asking if they'd like to join you: "I've been wanting to try out the new restaurant on San Fernando, and I wondered if you'd like to have dinner there with me Friday night."

- Don't share details or conversations from your new relationship with others. You are naturally excited about this complex, extraordinary, unique person you've met, but keep it to yourself for a while as a matter of respect for the other person. In addition, not everyone is eager to hear about your love life.

> *All the world loves a lover, but it usually runs away from him when he talks.*
> —FRANK MOORE COLBY

- Don't be brief when you are telling the other person how wonderful they are. "Brevity may be the soul of wit, but not when someone's saying, 'I love you.'" (Judith Viorst)

Be sure that the two of you are at the same level of feeling—telling someone that you love them or that they're wonderful when they don't want to hear it from you will embarrass both of you.

Special Situations

- Vary your "conversations" with letters and telephone visits. You will see each other in new ways when you have to put words on paper or when you can't actually see each other as you talk.

- If you are dating someone with whom you work, you have no doubt checked company rules about in-house dating and you have also no doubt made sure this relationship is worth the inherent risks. That said, you will want to strictly limit conversations between you during office hours. Strictly. Pretend that you work in different buildings several blocks apart and deal with the relationship that way. All conversation would thus take place outside work hours.

▶ If you are single and spend any time in public, you might become involved in conversations with unwelcome sexual messages, uncomfortable conversations that you neither seek nor wish to pursue. The action of choice is to remove yourself from the vicinity of this person with no boundaries, manners, or common sense. If you can't, move as far away as you can after saying something like:

> *The greatest sex toy ever invented may be the telephone. Sometimes there's nothing more erotic than a disembodied voice, no question more tantalizing than a whispered "What are you wearing?" Especially when you can make up the answer. On the phone your hair always looks great, your legs are always shaved, your worst pair of underwear becomes a silk negligee.*
> —MEGHAN DAUM

"Did I say or do something that led you to think you could talk to me like that?"

"Does your mother know how you behave?"

"I don't care for this conversation. You'll excuse me, I'm sure."

"I'm meeting a friend. Excuse me."

"I'm sorry, you must have mistaken me for someone else."

"You can't possibly think I like what you're saying."

> *Good conversation not only stirs ideas and the exchange of ideas, but it gives two persons a more vivid impression of each other.*
> —FRANCES BRUCE STRAIN

Topics of Conversation

After you have known the other person for some time there will probably be nothing you can't talk about together. Or, perhaps, you will have learned which topics are favorites and which are somewhat off-limits to the other person. But that's later.

In the beginning, the general idea is to choose topics that are comfortable and entertaining for both of you.

Topics to Consider

Anecdotes, opinions, observations

Animals: current and childhood pets, extinction of species, volunteer work with shelters

Books: recently read, favorites, childhood memories

Concerts and favorite music groups

Local-interest items: new museum, renovated sports arena, another mall going up, restaurant recommendation

Movies you've seen or liked or have seen more than once

Newspaper items: cartoon strip, editorial you like, oddity, ongoing situation

Setting: how crowded it is, how good the band is, how easy it is to hear oneself talk, how you enjoy playing pool, how good the food is

Sports: favorite sports activity, favorite spectator sport, favorite teams, sports you or they would like to take up

The Arts: theater, classical music, museums, ballet, opera, arts you or they enjoy doing

TV shows you or they never miss

Weather, if it's dramatic (record high or low temperatures, earthquakes, floods, blizzards)

What's exciting for you or them these days: current projects, hobbies, upcoming trips

Work life: what you or they enjoy about it; how you or they got into that field; how company cultures vary; career goals; similarities between your feelings about your work

> *Plenty of guys are good at sex, but conversation, now there's an art.*
> —Linda Barnes

Topics to Avoid

Bragging, one-upping, or putting down others

Controversial issues

Criticisms and complaints about family, work, government, life

Divorce—yours or theirs

Long, involved stories about your work, life, vacations, health

Money: income, possessions, how much things cost

Off-color jokes

Personal problems, failures, flaws

Politics

Reflections on other people present

Religion

Retelling movies and TV shows you've seen

Sex

The other person's dating history

Conversation Starters

Conversations between two people learning to like and then to love each other grow in a spiral. Some conversations after six months sound like some of the same conversations you had on your first date. But others could never have taken place then. Pace your conversation to your developing relationship.

Striking Up an Acquaintance: First Remarks

"Are you a member of the club? I'm a guest, and I've never been here before."

"Can we cut straight to the chase? Will you marry me?" (This one could bomb, but if you meet a kindred soul, it's a great way to start.)

"Does this music remind you of anything?"

"Do you know anything about the next speaker?"

"Do you know if there's a parking garage nearby? I had a hard time finding a parking place."

"Do you know many of the people here tonight?"

"Everyone seems to be having a good time."

"Excuse me, but where did you find the éclairs? I didn't see any."

> *Two things remain irretrievable: time and a first impression.*
> —Cynthia Ozick

"Excuse me, do you know the woman in the green dress? I think I should know her, but I'm blank at the moment."

"Excuse me, have you seen the guest book? It's supposed to be in this room, I think."

"Have you ever seen so many fresh flowers in your life? I understand they're all from the Malafairs' gardens."

"Hello. Is this seat taken?"

"Hello. My name is Maureen Ashanti. Is anyone sitting here?"

"Hello. This is a great engagement party. Will you be able to attend the wedding too?"

"Hi. Do you live around here? Maybe you know where I could mail a letter on my way home."

"Hi! My name is Brenda Foley, and I'm your host's sister. She told me to go mingle. How do you know Kate?"

"Hi. Say, do you think a person could slip out now, or would that be rude? I've got an early flight in the morning."

Not every conversation changes your life, but any conversation can.
—JULIE, LIZ, SHEILA, MONICA, AND LIAN DOLAN

"How are you involved in this organization?"

"How do you know Gineen?"

"I'm going back for more shrimp. Could I bring you a small plate of them?"

"I'm refilling my drink. May I bring you a fresh one?"

"I've always wanted to ask someone if it's true that strobe lights can trigger seizures in some people. Do you know?"

"John Lindsay suggested I come over and say hello to you, since we both have Italian greyhounds."

"Someone just told me we both work at the public library, but I've never seen you there. Where do you work?"

"The band is terrific. Do you know who they are?"

"This is my first time here. Is it always this crowded?"

"What do you think of the band?"

"What's your connection to this group?"

"Would you like to dance?"

Talking With Romance in Mind

Striking Up an Acquaintance: First Remarks Not to Make

"Don't I know you?" (If you really mean this, phrase it more originally so that it doesn't sound like a bad pickup line—for example, "I think our paths have crossed somewhere. Would it be at Calahan & Calahan, or perhaps at St. Luke's Episcopal Church, or perhaps in the Loring Park neighborhood?")

"Do you come here often?" (Nobody wants to admit that they do.)

"Do you have the time?" (Nearly everyone wears a watch.)

"Hello, I don't know any of you, but I'm practicing my mingling tonight." (This one might be okay sometimes, but it can also make people want to suggest you go practice somewhere else.)

"I'm no good with pickup lines but I find you attractive and I'd like to get to know you better." (I'll say you're not good with pickup lines!)

"My friend wants to meet you." (If it really is the friend, you don't want to know someone who can't do their own meeting; if this is pretext, what's up with that?)

"Say, are you by any chance seeing a psychiatrist? I thought I saw you in Dr. Chalmers' waiting room." (This does not require an explanation.)

"What brings you here?" (The same thing that brings you?)

> *If you never want to see a man again, say, "I love you, I want to marry you, I want to have children"—they leave skid marks.*
> —RITA RUDNER

"What do you think about this party?" (What's to think?)

"What's your sign?" (Outdated, but this can be asked later.)

"You look just like Mandy Moore/Jim Cazeviel." (Maybe later, if this is the truth, but it feels phony.)

"You look like a live wire. Mind if I join you?" (The other person will wonder all night what a live wire really looks like, and if that's a good thing.)

Striking Up an Acquaintance: Second Remarks

"An architect. Were you always interested in building things?"

"Did you read the article in *Newsweek* that mentioned that very thing?"

"Does your family live in town?"

"Do you, by any chance, play tennis?"

"Do you live in the area?"

"Do you work downtown?"

"Have you always lived here?"

"How did you get into that line of work?"

"I don't know a thing about metallurgy's applications today. Can you give me a little background?"

"That reminds me of 'Doonesbury'—did you read it this morning?"

"What are you looking forward to these days?"

"What do you do to keep so fit-looking?"

"What do you like to do on your days off?"

"What's your favorite holiday?"

"What's your work day like?"

Second and Third Dates

"Do you enjoy cooking?"

"Have you ever surfed?"

"How is your nephew—is he better?"

"How was your day today?"

"If you could see five bands from music history, which ones would they be?"

"Tell me more about how the mentoring program works."

"This morning I thought I saw you coming down the street, and for a moment I got so excited."

"What are five things you can't live without?"

"What are your all-time favorite movies? Why?"

"What first attracted you to that field?"

"What is the most boring situation you can imagine?"

"What's your dream job?"

"What's your favorite thing to do on a Sunday afternoon?"

"What was the last great book you read?"

"What would be a dream vacation for you?"

Later On

"How were we so lucky as to find each other?"

"I couldn't sleep last night—and you know why."

"I had a wonderful time Sunday. I haven't been on a Ferris wheel since I was a kid. You make my life a perpetual carnival."

"I keep thinking about the night we met."

"I love you." (This cannot be said too often. It isn't fancy, but it is powerful.)

"I still remember the first time I saw you."

"I thought of yet another reason I love you—this makes fourteen reasons in case you're keeping track."

"I've never told anyone this before, but I've always dreamed of ..."

"Just when I think I know everything about you, there's something new to admire."

"Not a minute goes by when I'm not thinking of you."

"One thing I'm looking forward to (besides seeing you again) is..."

"Remember the night we met?"

"There is no minute of the day when I'm not thinking of you."

"We are two of the lucky ones."

"When did you first realize I was the one?"

"Whenever I think of you, I feel like singing and dancing. Fortunately, especially when I'm at work, I don't."

"When I was little, I always hoped that when I grew up I'd..."

"You make me so happy!"

"You've become my whole world, and yet the whole world is more alive to me than ever before."

If They Say...You Say

If They Say	You Say
"Hey, Good Looking, do you want to dance?"	"Thank you, but I'm fine where I am."
"Tell me about yourself."	"That's a pretty tall order. Could you be more specific?"

"What are you doing tomorrow night?"	"I'm busy. And I think I should tell you that I foresee being busy for some time."
"May I call you?"	"You know what? There's a wonderful person out there somewhere waiting for wonderful you. But it's not me."
"Do you like "What if..." questions?"	"Do I! Let me start! What if you ..."
"You mentioned you play tennis. Would you like to play this weekend?"	"I'd love to. Shall we bring along a picnic lunch?"
"What sort of a person did you always dream you would end up loving?"	"Someone very like you, except that I obviously didn't think big enough because you are so much more than I could ever have imagined."
"I love you!"	"As much as I love you?"

Closing Lines

Saying "good-night" or "good-bye" can either be very hard or a great relief. If the latter, don't say anything that isn't true (for example, "I'll call you" or "Let's get together again soon"). As the sagacious and well-spoken Judith Martin ("Miss Manners") points out, "a person who doesn't feel rejected doesn't go away. A painless rejection isn't one." You naturally don't want to cause any more pain than necessary, but if you sense the other person wants to continue the relationship and you definitely do not, be clear that this is "good-bye" and not "good-night."

When You Want to Leave

"Good luck with everything you've got going on at work."

"Have a good life!"

"It's been nice meeting you. I hope life brings you success and happiness."

"Nice meeting you at last. I'm sure Jerry will let me know from time to time how you're doing."

"Take care of yourself now."

"Thanks for a nice evening. Now you can tell your mother we finally met."

"Thank you for the lovely evening. I'll never forget the ballet."

"Yes, well, good night."

When You Hate to Leave

"I can hardly wait for the time when we don't have to go back to our separate apartments."

"I don't know if I can wait until tomorrow to see you again!"

"I enjoy every minute of being with you."

"I know I'll see you again Friday night, but that seems like an eternity from now."

"It's only 4:00 in the morning. Do you want to go get an early breakfast?"

"Just a few minutes more, and then I really should go."

"Maybe I'd have another soda."

"Oh no! Four days and twenty hours until I see you again!"

"Thank you for a truly memorable day."

"This has been one of the nicest evenings I can remember."

"You don't have to leave just yet, you know."

"You'll be my last thought tonight and my first thought tomorrow morning."

Index

absolutes ("always," "never"), 81–82
"acting as if," 5–6, 24
advice, asking for inappropriately, 70, 84, 144
    giving, 83–84, 183, 196
air travel, conversations during, 158
"always," 81–82
answering machines, 166–168, 169–170
answers, close-ended, 45–47, 142
    one-word, 142, 197
apologies, 59–60, 62–66, 196
appreciation, 23–30, 103–104, 119–120, 181, 192, 205
argumentative individuals, 130–131
arguments, 68–70, 122–123, 198
attention, paying, 31, 34, 62, 119, 141, 144, 180, 181, 196
attitude, 3–4, 130

"bad"/"badly," 93
"basically," 93
betraying someone's secret, 64–65, 85
"between you and me," 85–86, 92
bigoted remarks, 58
blinking, 7
blunders. *See* faux pas
blushing, 7
body language, 7–9
bores, 75–76
bragging, 87–89, 142
business conversations, 99–113
business-social events, 129–138

Call Waiting, 170
candor, over-protesting one's, 84–85
celebrities, speaking with, 145–146, 160
cell phones, 118, 173, 207
children, talking about, 145
clichés, 182–183
complaining, 89, 121
compliments, giving, 23–27, 102, 157
    responding to, 29–30
"condolences," 183
conferences, 115–127
confidence, 4–5, 8, 115–116, 139–140
conflicts, 68–70, 122–122, 198
controversial subjects, 106–107, 130
conversational no-no's, 105–107, 120–121, 132–133, 143–145, 158–159, 170–171, 182–183, 196–198, 206–207
    predicaments, 61–73
    starters, 111, 124–125, 135–137, 149–151, 162–163, 175, 200–201, 210–214
conversations, unpleasant, 67
cultural issues, 9, 14, 58
dating, conversations while, 203–216
    someone from work, 207–208
death, 183–184
    miscarriages, 184
    of a co-worker, 184
    of a pet, 184
    stillbirths, 184
discretion, 87, 121, 131, 181, 207
distractibility, 8, 35

eating and drinking, 16, 131
egotism, 87–88, 132
embarrassment, how to deal with, 16
encouraging words and phrases, 40–41
ending a conversation, 19–22, 42–43, 72–73, 112–113, 126–127, 138, 152–153, 159, 164, 177, 189, 202, 215–216
errors, admitting, 119. *See also* faux pas
eye contact, 18, 205
family, talking with, 191–202
faux pas, 22, 116, 145
favors, denying, 184–186
　requesting, 172
feelings, sharing, 194
fidgeting, 7–8
filler words and phrases, 37–42
first names, using, 12, 108
foreign languages, 94
foreign travel, 9, 14
forgetting names, 61–62
"frankly," 84–85
friends, talking with, 191–202
fundraisers, 129, 133–134
funerals, what to say at, 183–184
generalizations, 81–83
gestures, 7–9
good-bye, saying, 21–22, 215–216
gossiping, 67–68, 86–87
grimaces, 7
hand-shaking, 13–14, 18
hold, putting caller on, 169
homeless, the, 160
"honestly," 84
"hopefully," 93
how to end a conversation, 19–22, 42–43, 72–73, 112–113, 126–127, 138, 152–153, 159, 164, 177, 189, 202, 215–216
how to start a conversation, 111, 124–125, 135–137, 149–151, 162–163, 175, 200–201, 210–214
hugs, 18–19
humor, 55–60, 65–66, 145
hurry syndrome, 140
hurting someone's feelings, 62–64
"I," using, 15, 88
ideas, sharing, 120–121
"if they say ... you say," 111–112, 125–126, 137–138, 151–152, 164, 176, 188–189, 201, 214–215
ignorance, confessing, 16
insulting someone, 62–64
interments, what to say at, 183–184
interrupting, 78–80, 100, 117, 144
　response to, 100, 117
introductions, 10–13
I-statements, 142
jargon, 16, 94, 132, 145
jokes, 55–60, 65–66, 145
　off-color, 58, 108, 124
　tasteless, 65–66
keeping a conversation going, 37–42
"like," 92
listening, 31–36, 38–39, 179, 180, 193
"literally," 92–93
love and conversation, 203–216
meetings, 115–127
"me too" problem, 17, 88–89
mingling, 19, 121
miscarriages, 184
misuse of words, 92–94
monologues, 42–43
monopolizing a conversation, 76–78, 143, 197
names, forgetting, 61–62
　remembering, 12
　using first names, 12, 108
name tags, 129
negativity, 105–106
networking, 133
"never," 81–82
nicknames, 12
no-no's, 105–107, 120–121, 132–133, 143–145, 158–159, 170–171, 182–183, 196–198, 206–207
off-color jokes, 58, 108, 124
one-liners, 56–57
one-upping, 87–89, 145
opening lines, 111, 124–125, 135–137, 149–151, 162–163, 175, 200–201, 210–214
parties, 139–153
perfectionism, 6
personal space, 9, 157
pet, death of, 184
platitudes, 182–183
pointing a finger, 9
positive, being, 3
posture, 6–7
principles of conversation, 14–19
public places, conversations in, 155–164
puns, 59
put-downs, 89–90
quarrels, 68–70, 122–123, 198
questions, 45–53, 123
　asking, 15, 45, 181, 193, 205
　close-ended, 45–47

questions (*Cont.*):
    good, 50–52
    inappropriate, 47–50, 70–71, 158
    intrusive, 48, 158
    open-ended, 45–47
    responding to, 52–53, 70–71
repetitive speech habits, 80–81
requests, turning down, 184–186
romance, conversations and, 203–216
saying "no," 184–186
secrets, telling, 64–65, 85
self-consciousness, 16
self-deprecation, 90–91
self-revelation, 14, 15, 142, 204
sentences, finishing others', 144
    not finishing, 94–95
sexual harassment/innuendo, 71–72, 208
shaking hands, 13–14, 18
shyness, 16, 206
silence, 71, 121, 143, 180–181
slang, 16
small talk, 17
smiling, 9
social events, 139–153
speakerphone, 170
speaking too loudly, 144
stillbirths, 184
subjects of conversation. *See* topics
suicide, sympathizing with survivors, 184

Swift, Jonathan, 95
sympathy, 108, 179–189
tact, 142, 193
talkative individuals, 19, 72–73, 107–108, 118
telephone conversations, 165–177
    business calls, 165–166, 169, 170–171
    consumer calls, 166
    followup acknowledgments, 160
    personal calls, 166
topics of conversation, 4, 108–109, 123–124,
    134–135, 146–148, 160–161, 173–175,
    186–188, 198–200, 205, 208–210
topics to avoid, 110, 124, 135, 148, 161,
    174–175, 187–188, 199–200, 209–210
topics to consider, 109–110, 123, 134–135,
    147, 160–161, 174, 187, 199, 209
touching, 18–19, 158
trouble, conversing with people in, 179–189
unpleasant conversations, 67
"utilize," 93
verbal tics, 80–81, 84–85
"what if" questions, 194–196, 206
wheelchair users, 157
"whoever"/"whomever," 93
"why?," 49–50
workplace conversations, 99–113
words, misused, 92–94
"you," using, 15
you-statements, 185

Index   221

About the Author

Rosalie Maggio (Frazier Park, California) is the author of 19 books, including *How to Say It: Words, Phrases, Sentences, and Paragraphs for Every Situation, Great Letters for Every Situation,* and *The How to Say It Style Guide.*